TOUR IN

SCOTLAND

TOUR
IN
SCOTLAND
1817

AND

OTHER MANUSCRIPT NOTES

BY

WASHINGTON IRVING

Edited with a Critical Introduction by

STANLEY T. WILLIAMS

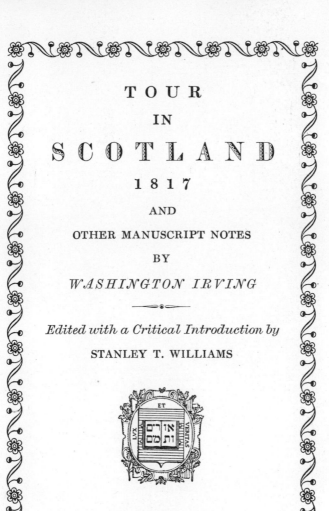

NEW HAVEN

YALE UNIVERSITY PRESS

MDCCCCXXVII

Copyright, 1927, by Yale University Press

Printed in the United States of America

TABLE OF CONTENTS

LIST OF ILLUSTRATIONS

ACKNOWLEDGMENT

———⋅◦⋅———

THE publication of this volume has been made possible through the kindness of Mr. Preston Davie, of Tuxedo Park, New York City, who loaned me, for transcription and editing, the two manuscript journals of Washington Irving's *Tour in Scotland*.

S. T. W.

INTRODUCTION

Washington Irving's *Tour in Scotland*, now
first published, has a biographical and literary
importance not possessed by his other journals
of travel. It was written at the very turning
point of his career, in the year 1817, the year
in which he was, perhaps, most strongly influ-
enced by Walter Scott, by Robert Burns, by
the literary society of England and Scotland,
and by old, romantic England. In this year and
in 1818 he absorbed and recorded materials not
only for *The Sketch Book*, but for some of his
most characteristic work in *Bracebridge Hall*,
The Crayon Miscellany, and *Wolfert's Roost*.
Three notebooks survive to tell the story of his
mental life in this creative period. The first,
a tiny pocket affair, *Notes while preparing
Sketch Book &c.*, is remarkable as the genesis
of a permanent work of literature; the second
and third are complementary to this more personal notebook in containing also the origins of
essays, but are of more interest to a layman,
since they are themselves literature. Irving's
records of his travel have always interest, and
these, informal, vivid, rich in atmosphere, and
touched with the latent power of the future essayist, may stand on our shelves beside the vol-

umes which the world has accepted. The *Tour in Scotland* itself resembles a posthumous Geoffrey Crayon essay, not unlike "Abbotsford" or "Newstead Abbey."

Perhaps the true diarist must have a hint of disorder. In traveling, to wait for quiet before writing means often to write when it is too late and does not matter. Irving wrote, it is certain, when and where the mood seized him. The price was, in many a notebook, confusion, obscurity, and illegibility; even, I sometimes suspect, for the essayist himself. Yet this price was nothing; from it we secure a spontaneous uncovering of his mind. The editor's task has been partly to restore some impression of order. This has been easy in the case of the two journeys. These are reproduced, with the exception of two or three obvious *arrière-pensées*, in Irving's sequence. The additional entries have been arranged under the head of *Fragments*. Such they are, and sequence has little value; besides, sequence is, from the condition of the notebooks, utterly indeterminable. No importance, then, has been attached, as in *Notes while preparing Sketch Book &c.*, to establishing the probable order of entries. The pocket volume is primarily a source book for a work of art; these two are miscellanies of travel and observation. The assembling, then, has been completed under the following captions: *Tour in*

Scotland, Excursion to Runcorn, and *Fragments.* Under the last are "Notes on the West and South," "The Story of Rosalie," and "Personalia: Reading, Writing, and Miscellaneous Notes." Out of the two journals has been made one book. Every legible word has been published, and the reader may reconstruct readily, if he desires, the original arrangement of the two notebooks by the figures in brackets preceding the entries. The larger notebook has been called "Volume I," the smaller "Volume II." Volume and page so indicated represent a definite paging of the manuscripts by the editor. By this arrangement the *Tour in Scotland* is not continually interrupted by an absurdly irrelevant phrase, such as a tavern bill; and Irving's reading, for example, during the year is by this regrouping made comprehensible. As a whole the two notebooks now tell a fairly coherent story.

Physically, these two manuscripts are interesting. Volume I, the larger notebook, is seven and three-sixteenths inches in length and four and seven-sixteenths in width. It is oblong, octavo, bound in limp sheep covers, and is written in both ink and pencil on unruled paper, for the most part on both sides of the folios. It contained at one time sixty-four folios or one hundred and twenty-eight pages. It has been rebound with paper slips, and the inside back

company with Wm C. Preston (since a Senator of the US)"; and "Memoranda made by Washington Irving of Sunnyside presented to me by my cousin Mrs P. M. Irving January 1885. George Irving." The following describes the interior of the notebook: pages 11, 12, 13, 14, 15, 16, 17, and 18 are apparently cut out close to the binding; 67, 68, 75, and 76 are almost wholly torn out; 1, 2, 3, 4 are slightly torn. These pages are blank or rubbed out: 4, 6, 28, 32, 38, 41, 60, 70, 84, 90, 99, 104, and 108. Sketches, inferior to those of the first volume, are on pages 19, 21, 25, 37, 40, 47, 50, 51, 54, 56, 72, and 79 (two sketches). As in the larger notebook, the pages of Volume II are unevenly filled, but by a computation similar to that in Volume I, the words total about seven thousand two hundred. This printed book, therefore, includes between sixteen and seventeen thousand words written by Irving, and hitherto unknown.[1]

In these two volumes the editor has employed procedures like those in connection with the small pocket volume. All entries have been reproduced, whenever legible, and these have been retained in their original spelling, punctuation, indentation, and capitalization. In the last points Irving is capricious, as in the matter

[1] The photostats of these two notebooks have been added to the collection of Irvingiana in the Yale University Library.

of dashes and periods, and his intentions cannot always be determined. His spelling of Scottish names is also erratic. He has crossed out numerous words and a few passages. In the first case his deletions, usually inconsequential, have not been reproduced, and the passages only when they seem significant. Some writing is hopelessly blurred and faint, but it has seemed best to reproduce as much of this as possible. All doubtful readings are queried. The annotation endeavors to explain facts concerning Irving, not those concerning Scottish history, which are easily accessible. It aims primarily to illumine Irving's mind during the years covered by the notebooks. Whenever more than one or two words have been decipherable, the passage has been printed. One illegible or obliterated word has been designated by a long dash. A blank space in the original has been so left in the book, and is referred to in the notes, as are illegible or rubbed out passages of more than one word. Dashes or lines between passages have been omitted. In the section called *Fragments* are various passages which were the original drafts of later essays. These drafts have been collated with the finished essays, and also with intermediate versions of earlier editions. They should be studied in conjunction with the more significant passages in *Notes while preparing Sketch Book &c.* All paging in reference to

Irving's essays is based on *The Works of Washington Irving*, Riverside edition, G. P. Putnam's Sons, New York, 1864, 1868, 1869. It is important to notice that in the three note-books, taken together, may be found germs of at least seventeen essays, namely: "Roscoe," "The Wife," "Rip Van Winkle," "Rural Life in England," "The Broken Heart," "The Widow and Her Son," "Rural Funerals," "A Sunday in London," "The Boar's Head Tavern, Eastcheap," "Westminster Abbey," "Philip of Pokanoket," "The Angler," "Horsemanship," "St. Mark's Eve," "Abbotsford," "The Creole Village," and "Mountjoy."

II

IT is tempting to imagine that Irving had long anticipated a tour in Scotland. He was half Scottish, his father, William Irving, having been a native of the Orkneys. On the first pilgrimage to Europe he had missed Scotland, and it was now more than two years since he had landed at Liverpool for his longest stay abroad.[1] He had traveled in England, Wales, France, and Italy. For scenery Scotland was superior to these, and superior to scenery in Scotland was its literary life: the past of Burns, and the present of Walter Scott. In Edinburgh, too, were

[1] For a summary of Irving's life in 1817 see *Notes while preparing Sketch Book &c.*, pp. 7, 8.

Jeffrey and the race of reviewers. Scott had given Irving in 1813 a most welcome tribute concerning Diedrich Knickerbocker's *A History of New York;* it was to Abbotsford that Irving hastened, with a letter from Thomas Campbell. Irving was thirty-four, no longer very young, and, despite the brief flare of *Salmagundi* and *A History of New York,* hardly renowned as a man of letters. He was poor; he had suffered grief; and his future, if one had asked his indulgent elder brothers, was considered problematical. Yet he was agreeable, gentlemanly, ambitious in his own way, and the regard for Scott and Jeffrey which took firm root during this tour was not unreciprocated. The student of the journals may discover in their pages a strong and delicate mind, and may supply for himself the blank space in the diary after the phrase "Scott himself appeared limping up the hill." The meeting was the commencement of a genuine friendship.[1]

Irving was in Scotland somewhat less than a month, from August 25 to September 21 or 22, 1817. Pierre Irving, the orthodox biogra-

[1] "When you see Tom Campbell," wrote Walter Scott, "tell him, with my best love, that I have to thank him for making me known to Mr. Washington Irving, who is one of the best and pleasantest acquaintances I have made this many a day." Letter to John Richardson, September 22, 1817. [J. G. Lockhart], *Memoirs of the Life of Sir Walter Scott, Bart.,* Edinburgh and London, 1837, IV, 87, footnote.

pher, devotes little space to this formative experience in his uncle's life, and makes no attempt to account for each day. This is worth doing, and the three notebooks made it possible. The long lists of Scotch names on pages 40, 41, 42, 43 indicate Irving's plans for his tour; the early pages detail the adventures of the days en route to Edinburgh and in the city; and others recount the trip by carriage and on foot among the Highlands. From the journals and other data has been reconstructed, not without difficulty, Irving's itinerary:

Thursday	August 21, 1817 8.30 a.m.	Left London
Monday	August 25 "About 12 Oclock" "After dinner"[1]	Arrived Berwick-on-Tweed Left Berwick-on-Tweed
	10 p.m.[2]	Arrived Edinburgh
Tuesday	August 26	Edinburgh
Wednesday	August 27	Edinburgh
Thursday	August 28	Edinburgh
Friday	August 29	Left Edinburgh Arrived Selkirk
Saturday	August 30	Left Selkirk Arrived Abbotsford
Sunday	August 31	Abbotsford
Monday	September 1	Abbotsford (Dryburgh Abbey)
Tuesday	September 2	Abbotsford
Wednesday	September 3	Left Abbotsford Arrived Edinburgh
Thursday	September 4	Edinburgh

[1] 2 p.m. See *Notes while preparing Sketch Book &c.,* p. 46.

[2] *Ibid.,* p. 47.

Friday	September 5	Edinburgh
Saturday	September 6	Edinburgh
Sunday	September 7	Left Edinburgh
		Arrived Linlithgow
		Left Linlithgow
		Arrived Falkirk
Monday	September 8 8 a.m.	Left Falkirk
		Arrived Stirling
Tuesday	September 9	Left Stirling
		Dunblane
		Arrived Perth
Wednesday	September 10	Kinnoul Hill
		Perth
		Left Perth
		Arrived Dunkeld
Thursday	September 11 6.30 a.m.	Left Dunkeld
		Balnaguard
		Aberfeldy
		Falls of Moness
		Taymouth
		Arrived Kenmore
Friday	September 12 7 a.m.	Left Kenmore
		Loch Tay
		Killin
		Loch Earn
Saturday	September 13 7 a.m.	Left Lochearnhead
		Arrived Callander
		Loch Katrine
Sunday	September 14	Inversnaid
		Arrived Tarbet
Monday	September 15 8.30 a.m.	Left Tarbet
		Loch Lomond
		Luss
		Arrived Dumbarton
Tuesday	September 16	Dumbarton
		Left Dumbarton
		Arrived Glasgow

Wednesday	September 17 7 a.m.	Left Glasgow
		Arrived Ayr
Thursday	September 18	Left Ayr
		Arrived Glasgow
		Left Glasgow
		Arrived Hamilton
		Arrived Lanark
Friday	September 19 8.30 p.m.	Left Lanark
		Arrived Edinburgh
Saturday	September 20	Edinburgh
Sunday	September 21	Left Edinburgh[1]

In Scotland from the first to the last day
Irving was a somewhat sentimental pilgrim.
Off Bamburgh he quotes Scott; at Alloway
Kirk he talks to the stone mason about Burns;
and he never wearies of seeing and sketching
the haunts of Rob Roy. Yet in Edinburgh he
gives us unconsciously a valuable picture of
life there in 1817. Dugald Stewart is out of

[1] The manuscript for these last two dates reads:
"Saturday 21" and "Sunday 22." But Irving's other
notes, such as "Sunday September 14," suggest that in
these entries he made an error either in the day of the
week or the day of the month. A letter quoted by Pierre
Irving (the original not accessible for verification) is
dated *Sunday,* September 22 (*Life and Letters of Washington Irving,* New York, 1862, 1863, 1864, I, 386). Yet
another letter (*ibid.,* I, 380) places September 1 as Monday. All the entries except these last two, September 21
and 22, confirm this arrangement of dates, the month of
September beginning on a Monday. An examination of
the calendar for the year 1817 proves that September 1
fell on Monday. It is impossible to say whether Irving
left Edinburgh on Sunday, September 21, or Monday,
September 22, though presumably his error was in the
day of the month, and he left the city on Sunday, September 21.

town, but he hears Francis Jeffrey talk, and on America, too. He meets Murray and old D'Iraeli; gleans news of Byron. The glimpse of Scott surrounded by his dogs is priceless. Jeffrey, more daring than some, avers that Scott wrote the Waverley novels; confesses they are the best things done in his time. Then there is sightseeing, the sightseeing we have all done: the Castle, the house of Knox, the pause at the stairs of Holyrood. Here Irving falls into a deeply characteristic mood: he feels himself interfused with the romantic past.

Yet he had, apart from the visit to Abbotsford, definite plans, and on September 7 he was in the chaise with William Campbell Preston, bound for Linlithgow. This Preston was an American, perhaps an old friend, but eleven years younger than Irving. He was the son of General Francis Preston, and the grandson of William Campbell, who commanded the American forces at the battle of King's Mountain. The time of the first meeting of Irving and Preston is uncertain. Tradition says it was at the White House, in Washington, in 1813, when young Preston was the guest of President and Mrs. Madison.[1] Preston's friendship with Irving was

[1] This tradition is at variance with a statement that Irving first met Preston in London in 1815 or later. See the article signed "A.M." (Mrs. Virginia Preston Carrington, niece and adopted daughter of W. C. Preston), in the magazine called *The Land We Love*, August, 1868.

enduring. Irving, it is said, introduced him to
Scott; and a story exists that both Preston
and Irving were guests of the Duke of Bed-
ford at his country-house over one Christmas
week. This was not the first excursion of the
two friends; they had met in June of this year
in Liverpool and had taken a holiday at Runcorn. In the fall of 1832 Irving again saw
Preston in Columbia, South Carolina; on
March 17, 1842, he dined with him, then a
United States Senator, in Washington; and
in the year of Irving's death (1859) they were
still in correspondence. Just now, however, Preston was more than a distinguished man; he was
twenty-three and an excellent traveling companion.[1]

The tour in the Highlands speaks for itself. There was good company, good weather,
and some hearty laughter. There was musing
over ancient castle and storied mountain, and,
as usual in Irving's narratives, plenty of time:
time for conversation with old peasants and for
watching the crows wheeling lazily overhead,
time to mourn that Dunblane had "not a handsome woman in it."[2] There are allusions to politics and wars, but merely to those dim romantic
contests of long ago: Queen Mary, Bannock-

[1] See references to William C. Preston on pp. 55, 56;
75-79; 125, 127.
[2] See p. 49.

burn, or Philiphaugh. We are struck in the description of the humanitarian establishment at Runcorn with Irving's singular indifference to the great contemporary issues in British and Scottish life which Brooke's protesting, philosophical cult suggests. Irving's mood is that described in the opening pages of *The Sketch Book:* the American musing over the past of old Britain. This intimates a tepid mind, but the contrary is true. One has only to notice the skill in the portraiture of the Caledonian characters, the unerring, deft selection of details from the lovely landscapes, the recording of the apt Scottish phrases, to see that Irving's mind at thirty-four is not mild, but shrewd; not vaguely sentimental, but alert for shades of character or setting,—in brief, the mind of the born observer of men and manners.

III

THE phrase on the inside cover of Volume II, "Most of the memoranda," suggests Irving's custom of returning to blank pages in his old notebooks. Except for the journeys in the Highlands and to Runcorn all items in the journals must be dated by internal evidence. One entry hints at the year 1807 or 1809. Many jottings were put down in 1817. Thus he writes "Coleridges new works Sybilline Leaves Biographia Literaria." These books appeared in 1817. Yet if, as seems likely, the comments on the Missouri and Mississippi were the result of observation, then these were written in 1832, and the notebooks crossed the Atlantic and went west with him. By similar reasoning some of the drafts of the essays in *The Sketch Book* (1819-1820) were written before these dates. Thus the fragments throw light on Irving's life during 1817, and also on later years.

The value of these is not less, but different. They tell us many things worth knowing about Washington Irving. The passages on the West and South show, as do the rough manuscript notes of *A Tour on the Prairies*,[1] his first-hand reactions to an America that must have seemed strange to the former young beau of New York and Philadelphia and the cosmopolitan, Europeanized author of *The Sketch Book*. The drafts of "The Widow and Her Son" or "St. Mark's Eve" are the beginnings of finished essays in the accepted manner of English literature about the year 1820. The little items on books are unique because they break Irving's customary silence about his reading. The wealth of Irving's general reading and culture has never been properly valued. Such notes confirm the suspicion that he was a master of certain kinds of poetry, and reveal his patient explora-

[1] In the Isaac N. Seligman Collection, New York Public Library.

tion of obscure writers. A list of reading compiled from the letters of Washington Irving would be short. Yet in his journals he unceasingly noted down the names of books which were influencing him. In passing, note the mode of literary criticism (on Leigh Hunt and Byron) of which he, with his age, was a victim. Besides the poetry of Burns and Scott, Irving is reading about this time Richard Hooker's *Ecclesiastical Polity*, Sir William Temple's *Of the Different Conditions of Life and Fortune*, Byron, Coleridge, and Shakespeare. In addition there are the puzzling passages, half-literary, half-autobiographical, such as that on loneliness, which indicate how closely knit in his mind were personal melancholy and the transmutation of this into literature.

Perhaps the notation most profitable for study is the curious fragment called "Rosalie." Into this are woven his own intimate feelings, and his literary ambitions in a field into which he had, finally, the good sense not to wander. No one believes that Washington Irving could have written a good novel. Yet the story of Rosalie hints that he wished to do so. The creator of "Buckthorne and His Friends" and "Mountjoy" was not altogether a writer of essays and short stories. We have recently learned that he aspired to become a dramatist. Perhaps, after all, this is the value of these notebooks: in them Washington Irving does not appear as in our histories of literature, a neatly classified writer, but volatile, impressionable, uncertain; reaching out, like all of us, to learn what may be the meaning of his mind.

I.

TOUR IN SCOTLAND

TOUR
IN
SCOTLAND

‖‖

[I, 7] 1817. Aug 21.[1]

LEFT London[2] at ½ past 8 a.m. in the
Smack Lively, Capt Wm Nesbitt, for Berwick on tweed.

I found the cabins crowded with men
women & children, evidently of the inferior
order—Weather rainy & uncomfortable.
Wind ahead—Felt rather disheartened at
the prospect of a long, disagreeable voyage,
in bad company: was consoled however by
meeting with a fellow passenger more unhappy than myself. This was a respectable
looking man, middle age—brown surtout-

[1] For Irving's itinerary and an account of his stay in
Scotland see Introduction, pp. 9-15. This entry, on page
7 of the notebook, is preceded by various jottings, such
as addresses and bills. For these and other scattered
entries see Note on the Fragments, pp. 132-136.

[2] The exact dates of Irving's stay in London are not
known. He arrived there from Liverpool about August
1, and remained some three weeks. This note establishes
the date of his departure from London. The entry should
be compared with his letter to Peter Irving, dated
Edinburgh, August 26, 1817. See *Life and Letters of
Washington Irving*, I, 376-380.

drab breeches & gaiters. umbrella & cane- He
stood on the after part of the deck with a
most unhappy aspect, watching the motley
throng that was continually augmenting on
board the smack. The corners of his mouth
were drawn down, his nose contracted, and
there was a glance of indwelling misery from
his eye and an ejaculated pish! whenever any
thing went wrong or a new passenger arrived.
Learned afterward that his name is Trotter,[1]
native of Edinburgh—at present residing on
the banks of a small stream that runs into the
Tweed about 13 miles above Berwick. [I, 8]

Another passenger that I found compan-
ionable was a scotchman about 30 who had
been much abroad, particularly in the Medi-
terranean—was well informed: somewhat
waggish and very entertaining.

We had on board a huge, broad shouldered
round bellied man about 55 years of age—
named Isaac Allison: from Alnwick in Northumberland. He is a master fisherman, owns
part in several vessels, and has probably been
a desperate smuggler in his time. He has evidently been a powerful, active man; his limbs
even now are well proportioned and indicate

1 This traveling companion and Isaac Allison, Irving
mentions again on pp. 23, 24, 26, 125, 130.

great strength. He was dressed in an old black coat; with huge skirts and unfathomable pockets—a black waistcoat—olive velvet breeches and black worsted stockings—after we set sail he exchanged his black coat for a snuff colored cloth Jacket—which he buttoned tight round his immense carcass. He was an incessant smoker. He had been to London to assist the cause of his son; who was master of a smuggling vessel that had lately a [I, 9] desperate conflict with a revenue vessel, in which several were killed in both sides. the Smugglers were acquitted it appearing that the revenue vessel fired twice into them without shewing colours.

Old Allison had the true Northumbrian burr and pronounced *r* like *ur*—

Our captain was a stout, healthy looking fellow of 40. with ruddy cheeks, blue eyes— an aquiline nose, and curley [*sic*] yellowish hair—a face indicating a fellow that had been full of frolick & wenching in his younger days.

There was also an old highlander on board of the name of Willie Symes; who had tended herds on the Grampian Hills. He was a singular compound of simplicity and cunning.

He had the broad Scotch accent & dialect,

and told us he had seen Norvals[1] grave, and
Macbeths castel [*sic*]— That he had had
mony a crack[2] wi the present Laird o' Dunsinane, who is as himmil[3] a body as eer you saw
in aa your life—He will talk wi a puir body
jist like an auld wife, an yet he has an awfu
knowledge o' the Law."[4]

[I, 10] The old man was a firm believer
in Witches fairies and warlocks. "Not that
theyre owr plenty nowadays; but they
abounded in auld times, when the world was
in Obscurity before the Scriptures had broke
out any thing great."

Old Allison and one or two other passen-
gers were full of their pranks upon the old
grampian hero. Hiding away his mull[5] at
which he at length got very wroth—though

---

1 Compare *Notes while preparing Sketch Book &c.*, p.
61, and this volume, p. 52.

2 Chat.

3 Probably Irving's version of "hummil," Scottish
form of "humble." Perhaps Irving misspells a form of
"hamald," meaning homely or domestic. See *The English
Dialect Dictionary*. The word occurs again on p. 52.

4 Willie Symes' anecdote of the Laird of Dunsinane
is ascribed, apparently, with very slight changes, to
Scott's caretaker, Johnny Bower. See "Abbotsford,"
The Crayon Miscellany, p. 250. Part of this passage is
quoted in [J. G. Lockhart] *Memoirs of the Life of Sir
Walter Scott, Bart.*, IV, 90.

5 Snuff-box. See A. Warrack, *A Scots Dialect Dictionary*, London and Edinburgh, 1911. Irving repeats the
last phrases of these two paragraphs. See p. 52.

they tried to persuade him there must be some witchcraft in it and that there was something "no canny about the box."

The first two days of our voyage were tedious—with rain & head winds. On Sunday 24th we had a fine fresh breeze and the vessel ploughed bravely through the waters—Fine sunny afternoon and moonlight night.

Monday morning Aug 25. Fine smacking breeze—vessel goes at the rate of 9 miles an hour. Have an indistinct view of the Northumbrian coast, shrouded in clouds & mist. As the day [I, 11] advances they break away. See the village of —— at a distance—Then Dunstanborough castle, on a rocky height

> And next they crossed themselves to hear
> The whitening breakers sound so near,
> Where boiling through the rocks they roar
> On Dunstanboroughs cavernd shore.
>
> *Marmion*[1]

We afterwards passed near to Bamborough castle; which stands bleakly and with an air of wild solitary grandeur on the sea coast.

[1] Irving's quotation, except for punctuation and spelling, is accurate. See *The Complete Poetical Works of Sir Walter Scott,* Cambridge edition, New York [1900], p. 101, "Marmion," Canto Second, lines 144-147. This and the succeeding passage from the poem are quoted together in the letter to Peter Irving. See *Life and Letters of Washington Irving,* I, 377.

Opposite to it is a picturesque island called Fearne [Farne] island.

> Thy tower proud Bamborough marked they there
> King Idas castle, huge & square
> From its tall rock look grimly down
> And on the swelling ocean frown.
>
> Marmion [*sic*]—[1]

From hence we were wafted on past Holy Island; scene of the trial of Constance de Beverly [*sic*] in Marmion.[2] Saw the remains of the Monastery of St Cuthbert: now apparently converted into a[3] of residence either for fishermen or for those who watch the beacons. [I, 12] About 12 Oclock we arrived at Berwick—[4]

Dangerous entrance to the harbour. Long mole of Stone erecting—The Tweed is here crossed by a long & picturesque bridge built by one of the James's. Stopped at the Red Lion. Mr Trotter accompanied me in a ramble about the old walls of the town. Fine view from an angle of the old works. See the town

---

[1] "Marmion," Canto Second, lines 148-151.

[2] *Ibid.*, Canto Second, lines 381-634.

[3] The words "some sort" have been crossed out by Irving.

[4] Compare this date, August 25, 1817, and the description of the journey through Lothian, with the references in the small notebook, *Notes while preparing Sketch Book &c.*, pp. 44-47.

FARNE ISLAND AND BAMBURGH CASTLE

& port below you—with the bridge stretching
across the river—the Northumbrian Hills beyond—and a wide expanse of ocean on the
other side the Tweed winding between naked
banks. Old watch towers on the side of the
town towards Scotland.

After dinner I left Berwick in a coach for
Edinburgh.[1] Pass through Dunbar.[2]

See an old border town near the road; and
the ruins of Traprain Convent at the foot of
the singular hill of that name the top of
which was coverd with clouds.

[I, 13] Road winds through solitary, naked
hills—possessing something of the stern
bleakness of Welsh scenery—then through
the rich fields of Lothian loaded with grain—

Arrive at Edinburgh late at night[3]—
Night stormy with heavy rain. Put up at
MacGregors Hotel Princes Street.

Tuesday 26. After Breakfast cross to the
old town. The morning bright & sunny, with

[1] The hour was two o'clock. See *Notes while preparing
Sketch Book &c.*, p. 46.

[2] No attempt has been made to annotate the places
visited by Irving, except in cases of personal or literary
interest. Irving's route was, on the whole, that of the
ordinary tourist. Accounts of the towns, lakes, and mountains, with their historical associations, are easily found.
For this reason, and for reasons of space, such explana-
tions are not included.

[3] 10 P.M. See *Notes while preparing Sketch Book &c.*,
p. 47.

large masses of clouds that give fine variety
of light & shade. Edinburgh remarkably picturesque & romantic in its general appearance. Smoke rising from houses between new
& old town, & lighted up by the morning sun,
gives a fine aerial effect to the rock & castle
& throws the old town into masses.

Constable,[1] *the Booksellers Shop*—a dark
low, dingy shop—I passed it at first without
noticing it, expecting to find a spacious, striking book shop—NB. [?] *Murrays*[2] *shop* is
equally unimposing tho' more fashionably
situated & elegant in its [I, 14] air. Murray
has a sign up—

Calton Hill—Magnificent Panorama from
it. The old & new town below you on one side
—Holy rood house & the romantic height of
Arthurs seat on another—& the Forth & wide
expanse of water on another.

1 Archibald Constable (1774-1827), forty-three years
old, was publisher for Scott and just now of great influence in the world of books. Scott discussed with him in
1819 the possibility of publishing *The Sketch Book.* As
early as July, 1825, Irving was approached by Constable
to write a biography of George Washington. See *Life and
Letters of Washington Irving,* I, 382, 384, 386, 442, 443;
II, 238, 249; IV, 292.

2 Irving's friendly relations with John Murray, the
famous publisher, continued until the latter's death in
1843. See *Notes while preparing Sketch Book &c.,* p.
82, and *Life and Letters of Washington Irving, passim.*

Dined with Mr Jeffrey, Mrs Renwicks[1] brother

Wednesday 27th Charlotte Square, the finest Square in Edinburgh—

The new town of Edinburgh is quite distinct from the old & merely connected by Bridges—It is the drawing room, the other the office—The fashionable world all reside together—and are quite brought into each others neighbourhood—The streets are so spacious, clean & well paved that there is no need of wheel carriages for the purposes of fashionable visiting—

Walked out with Mr John Jeffrey to his brother Francis Jeffreys[2] to dinner—roman-

---

[1] Mrs. Renwick was Jane Jeffrey Renwick, widow of William Renwick, of New York. Irving had been on intimate terms with the family. See G. S. Hellman, *Washington Irving, Esquire,* New York, 1925, pp. 50, 51, 53, 81, 90, 93; and, in particular, *Letters from Washington Irving to Mrs. William Renwick, and to her son, James Renwick, Professor of Natural Philosophy at Columbia University, written between September 10th, 1811 and April 5th, 1816.* Printed for private distribution, n.p., n.d.

[2] John Jeffrey, the younger brother of Francis Jeffrey, was a merchant. Francis Jeffrey (1773-1850) was now forty-four years old and the distinguished editor of the *Edinburgh Review.* He had been in America from October 7, 1813, to January 22, 1814, but did not meet Irving until the latter's visit to him. For accounts of Jeffrey's journey and his opinions on America, which supplement those vouchsafed to Irving, see Lord Cockburn, *Life of Lord Jeffrey with a Selection from his*

tic views of Edinburgh from different parts of the road.

[I, 15] Jeffrey has a lease for 32 years of a property held in mortmain about 3 miles from Edin[bg] called craigcrook. It is a very old Mansion—near 300 years old built of stone, in the castellated form with tower & turrets—very picturesque—situated at the foot of a beautiful range of well wooded hills —Jeffrey has made great additions & improvements to the house and is ornamenting the grounds with great taste.

Jeffrey very pleasant & hospitable in his own house, & apparently very amiable & happy in his domestic character.

Speaking of America, Jeffrey observed that he found more Luxury, & comfort in the style of living than he had expected. Disliked the virulent political discussions that prevailed at table—the Violent party feeling that prevented gentlemen of different parties

Correspondence, second edition, Edinburgh, 1852, I, 246; II, 49, 147, 183-185, 188, 372, 381. Irving's acquaintance with Jeffrey continued. See *ibid.,* II, 200-205. In comparison with Irving's opinion of Jeffrey, note Jeffrey's of Irving: "Washington Irving is rather low spirited and silent in mixed company, but is agreeable, I think, tête à tête, and is very gentle and amiable. He is a good deal in fashion, and has done something to deserve it. I hope you do not look on him in America as having flattered our old country improperly." *Ibid.,* letter to Mrs. Colden, of New York, Mardocks, May 6, 1822, II, 206.

from associating. Thinks our girls brought into company too early—makes them flippant & ignorant. Seems to have been most pleased in N. Y. with Wells[1] & P. A. Jay.[2] The former did not say much but talked well —The latter seemed frank & independent in his opinions and found fault promptly with any thing or person he did not like—[I, 16] Jeffrey delighted with Scotts novels[3]—thinks them the best things that have appeared in his time.

There seems to be no doubt here that Scott is the author. It is said that Scott has traversed over the ground of all his novels & has lived among the people, diligently drawing characters & manners. He is described by J as being Social, Joyous, full of anecdote of irrepressible good spirits, picturesque & mimic not over fastidious in his taste for story telling fond of a broad joke occasionally & quite a merry hearted man—[I, 17]

Thursday 28th   Visit Edinburgh castle.

[1] Probably John Wells (1770-1823), distinguished lawyer and controversialist.

[2] Peter Augustus Jay (1776-1843), lawyer, jurist, and state legislator.

[3] In 1817 the following novels of Scott had appeared: *Waverley,* 1814; *Guy Mannering,* 1815; *The Antiquary,* 1816; *The Black Dwarf,* 1816; *Old Mortality,* 1816. Jeffrey had reviewed *Waverley* in the *Edinburgh Review.*

Scarcely any part of the old building left. Barracks of Stone built at great expense and in deplorably mistaken style.—Grecian style —Had they been castellated they would have given a grand finish to this warrior rock.

Passing thro high street see the window from which Knox[1] held forth—Also the windows of the attic room, seven stories high where Hume[2] wrote the history of England—

Holyroodhouse. Queen Marys rooms the effect in thus treading on the heels of antiquity—seems to obliterate the space of time between us—as if we hear the very sound of the steps of former ages—like Pompeii—

Different pictures of poor Mary in her different periods of life—rich crimson when young & happy in france—Black when dressed for Execution

[I, 18] Dined at Jeffreys. Was disappointed in not meeting with Dugald Stewart.[3]

[1] The house is on High Street, beyond South Bridge Street. It is wrongly believed that John Knox (1505-1572) lived here from 1560 to 1572.

[2] Irving probably means David Hume's (1711-1776) "familiar home in St. James's Court; in the Launmarket." See Henry Calderwood, *David Hume,* Edinburgh and London, 1898, p. 154. The *History of England,* Volume I, appeared in 1754; Volume II in 1756; Volumes III and IV in 1759; and the remaining volumes in 1761.

[3] Dugald Stewart (1753-1828), the philosopher. "Jeff-

His Wife & Daughter were there, but he was prevented by some circumstance from coming. Mrs Stewart is author of the beautiful Song—*"The tears I shed must ever fall"*[1]— Of the party were—

Lady Davy[2] formerly Mrs Apreece—a

rey tells me I am lucky in meeting with Dugald Stewart, as he does not come to Edinburgh above once in a month." Letter to Peter Irving, Edinburgh, August 26, 1817, *Life and Letters of Washington Irving,* I, 376-380. Another letter to Peter from Abbotsford, on September 1, mentions his disappointment in not seeing Stewart. *Ibid.,* I, 380.

[1] The first of the five stanzas of this song reads:

> The tears I shed must ever fall;
> I weep not for an absent swain,
> For time can past delights recall,
> And parted lovers meet again.
> I weep not for the silent dead.
> Their toils are past, their sorrows o'er
> And those they loved their steps shall tread,
> And death shall join to part no more.

Robert Burns composed the first four lines of the last stanza. Miss Cranston, who wrote the song, became in 1790 the second wife of Dugald Stewart. See *Notes on Scottish Song By Robert Burns, written in an interleaved copy of the Scots Musical Museum with Additions by Robert Riddell and Others,* edited by J. C. Dick, London, 1908, p. 59.

For information concerning this song I am indebted to Mr. William Corner and Mr. D. Wilson, both of Glasgow.

[2] The wife of Sir Humphry Davy (1778-1829), the natural philosopher. "Lady Davy was in excellent spirits, and talked like an angel. In the evening when we collected in the drawing-room, she held forth for upwards of an hour; the company drew around her and seemed to listen in mute pleasure; even Jeffrey seemed to keep his colloquial powers in check to give her full chance. . . ." *Life and Letters of Washington Irving,* I, 380.

belle esprit. Talks charmingly—was full of anecdote of the french court, both Bonapartes and Bourbon.

Madame La Voisser[1] late Comtess de Rumford—a hideous, coarse featured, ill dressed, fiercely painted woman, but apparently good humoured & full of spirits.

Dubruyl [?] Daniel [?] Minister of Irish extraction—Polite old Gentleman & smoothly spoken.

Lord Webbe Seymour, man of model & simple manners & appearance; amiable manners; very fond of Geology—

Mr. Underwood, who was for many years a detenu [?] in france which he says has made him good for nothing for the rest of his life—having forced upon him idle habits—

[I, 19] Mr Murray a solicitor—&c—

Rogers[2] the poet, when in Italy was called

---

[1] For further account of persons at this dinner, see *Life and Letters of Washington Irving,* I, 379-382.

[2] Irving knew Samuel Rogers (1763-1855) as early as 1820. Their friendship continued until the poet's death in 1855. As late as December 8, 1852, Irving gave H. T. Tuckerman a letter of introduction to Rogers. "He is a man," he wrote Tuckerman, "*I love and honor." Ibid.,* IV, 92. The entire history, still unwritten, of Irving's relations with Rogers, includes interesting facts concerning the former's debts to English society and English poetry. References to Rogers occur in unpublished letters of Irving, and various meetings are mentioned in the *Life and Letters of Washington Irving.* See II, 24,

by the servants *Rogero*—at another place
Heavino [?] *de* [?] *Memoria*—

He is very pale & meagre and has a doleful
appearance—at one watering place or country party he complained of the place being so
full that he could not find where to lay his
head—a wag demanded—cant he find a
church yard?—

Murray told a story of a party at Mr
Kelleys—a relative [?] of Lord Kellys—in
former days when the conviviality of the
table was carried to great excess. The party
had been at hard drinking for two or three
days—when one of the party regarding another on the other end of the table for some
time—who was leaning back in his chair, his
eyes fixed, his jaw fallen—requested the person next the other to jog his neighbor for
he looks so gash[1] I fear a is na canny wi him
—Hoot mon says the other hes been dead
these twa hours but I thought best not to
mention it as it might mar good company.

[I, 20] Murray told a still more extrava-
gant story of a nother [*sic*] family famous
in the olden time for good living. They kept

82, 87, 195, 196, 197, 198, 203, 204, 208, 251, 475, 477;
III, 105, 116, 196, 309; IV, 91, 92, 221, 320.

[1] Grim, or ghastly.

open house. The scene [?] was always going on—A punch bowl of mighty dimensions was never suffered to be empty and all comers were welcome—the family relieved each other and there was a perpetual session—One day a stranger, as was customary, rode up to the portal gave his horse in charge to a servant until he should refresh himself, and took his seat at the hospitable board. So well he liked the cheer that there he sat—day after day, month after month—year after year—until taking umbrage at something that occurred —he called a servant & ordered his horse in high dudgeon—troth your honour replied the latter your steeds been dead these three years—

[II, 78] Roslyn [Roslin] castle[1] sundown Daws & swallows sporting in the air view of the Lyne—Sun setting behind the pentland hills

Old woman at the Abbey.   fine situation of the castle—as they never built their castles till they went around the country to get a fine situation

[1] Irving may have visited Roslin on any of the days passed in or near Edinburgh: August 26, 27, 28; September 4, 5, or 20. This notation from Volume II has been placed beside the other records of Edinburgh and its vicinity.

Dwarf about 3 feet high —
met at the foot of ———— brae
helped him over a style — an
old man. large head — long body
short legs. ————————————
——————— a ragged ——— little
———— apron. ———————
———— he was a ———— wheel-
wright. ———— in Edinburgh
——— going to St Anthony's well
to drink the water — was ——
———— to go ———— but it
rained. ———— to go but had not
———— for a long time. ———— with
———— of an ———— a cliff. ————
the ———— of St Anton's chapel

THREE DRAWINGS OF THE DWARF

[II, 19] Dwarf[1] about 3 feet high met at the foot of arthurs seat helped him over a style—an old man—large head—long body short legs—rusty wig shewing stuff beneath a ragged hat—blue coat little leathern apron, blue trousers found he was a spinning wheel wright—resident in Edinburgh was going to S[t] Antonys well to drink the water—was minded to go yesterday but it rained—used often to go but had not been for a long time —pointed to the ruins on a cliff. It was the ruins of S[t] Antonys [?] chapel [II, 20] it must have been a weary way to go to do penance. Well a little stream that trickles from the side of a rock into a small basin & a cup firmly fastened by a chain little man drinks my health I returned the compliment & we parted he returning me many thanks—[2]

> Here lyes ane honorabil
> Voman callit Marjorit
> Erskine[3]

[1] Irving begins the page with three pencil sketches of the dwarf. Following the entry, on the opposite page (II, 21) is a pencil sketch of Arthur's Seat.

[2] A memorandum of five words, following this entry, begins: "Monument . . ." and is thereafter illegible. These are possibly names from Greyfriars' Churchyard, in Edinburgh. Compare p. 130, footnote 9.

[3] Apparently an inscription, or an epitaph.

[II, 80] Contrast feelings awakened in visiting Scotland with those of Italy[1]

Scotch situations [?] come nearer to my heart. witching songs of the nursery earliest days of my childhood—my puir buried sister—[2] auld lang syne—nothing remarkable in scenery of the country to the luxuriant scenery I have beheld—but they have tied [?] the charms of poetry on every river [?] hill & grey rock made [?] the desart to blossom as the rose—

[1] This passage has been transferred from the second volume of notes. Irving left New York for France on May 19, 1804. On June 25 his vessel reached the mouth of the Gironde, where it was quarantined. He reached Genoa, after a journey in southern France, about the third week in October. On April 14, 1805, he left Rome for Paris. He set out from Milan on May 2, and arrived in Paris on May 24. He embarked at Gravesend on January 18, 1806, for America, and was in New York some sixty-four days later (March 23, 1806). This journey produced, directly, no literature, and Irving mentions in a letter his comparative irresponsiveness to Italy. *Life and Letters of Washington Irving,* IV, 258. For an account of this voyage to America and the years immediately following, see Diedrich Knickerbocker's *A History of New York,* edited by Stanley Williams and Tremaine McDowell, New York [1927], Introduction, ix-xxviii.

[2] Irving's father, William Irving, was Scottish, a native of Shapinsha, one of the Orkney Islands. Seven of Washington's ten brothers and sisters lived to mature age. One child of William and Sarah Irving was buried in England in 1762 or 1763, Irving may here allude to this loss, or to the death of another sister in 1808. See *Life and Letters of Washington Irving,* I, 217.

—old buildings—clothed with poetry as with ivy—

[I, 94] Aug. 30. Saturday. Leave Selkirk after an early Breakfast, for Melrose.[1] The road lay along the side of hills in view of the Tweed—which is a clean stream without any trees, and running between naked grey Hills.

About 4 miles from Selkirk the chaise stopped at the gate of Abbots Ford; Mr. Scotts country residence. The road overlooks his house & grounds, which are situated on the declivity of a Hill at the foot of which runs the Tweed. I sent the postillion with a letter of Introduction from Mr Thomas Campbell,[2] and a card requesting to know whether it would be agreeable for Mr Scott

[1] Compare the opening pages of "Abbotsford," *The Crayon Miscellany.* See also letter to Peter Irving, Abbotsford, September 1, 1817, *Life and Letters of Washington Irving,* I, 380-382. The date, as here written, does not coincide with later dates recorded by Irving. See Introduction, pp. 10-12, for Irving's itinerary in Scotland.

[2] The letter of August 26 to Peter refers to this "very particular letter to Scott from Campbell," with whom Irving became acquainted soon after his arrival in England in 1815. See *ibid.,* I, 203, 204, 230, 253, 299, 303, 305, 334, 335, 344, 364, 365, 371, 378, 380, 387; II, 421; III, 21; IV, 322. See the long letter written by Irving on his friendship with Campbell, *Life and Letters of Thomas Campbell,* edited by William Beattie, New York, 1850, xi-xvi. See also Cyrus Redding, *Literary Reminiscences and Memoirs of Thomas Campbell,* London, 1860, pp. 352, 353.

to receive a visit from me in the course of the day.[1] The noise of the chaise & the appearance of the postillion had given the alarm to a legion of dogs that garrison Scotts castle: all their throats were opened and one black greyhound mounted on a wall seemed to lead the chorus.

In a few minutes Scott himself appeared limping up the hill.[2]

[II, 22]   Linlithgow[3]
             Stirling
             Callander

[1] "Scott's family," says his biographer, "well remember the delight with which he received this announcement— he was at breakfast, and sallied forth instantly, dogs and children after him as usual, to greet the guest, and conduct him in person from the highway to the door." [J. G. Lockhart], *Memoirs of the Life of Sir Walter Scott, Bart.,* IV, 88.

[2] Allusions to the visit to Scott may be found in *Notes while preparing Sketch Book &c.,* pp. 83-85. Compare also *Life and Letters of Washington Irving,* I, 381-384; "Abbotsford," *The Crayon Miscellany,* pp. 243-319; and [J. G. Lockhart], *Memoirs of the Life of Sir Walter Scott, Bart.,* IV, 87-95. Lockhart notes Irving's error in assigning 1816 as the year of the visit. See *The Crayon Miscellany,* No. 2, Philadelphia, 1835, p. 1. This error was corrected in later editions.

[3] This list of places and that on pp. 42, 43, should be compared with the itinerary reconstructed on pp. 10-12. In the account of his journey Irving does not mention Cairndow, Amulree, Cupar, Kinghorn, Carnwath, or Blair.

Loch Catrine
   Then
Cross to Lochlomond
   Mr Buchanan[1]
Inverary [Inveraray]
Cairndow
   to
Lochearnhead
Crieff
Amulree
Dunkeld
Perth
Dundee
Cupar Fife

[II, 23]   Kinghorn
Leith ——
   from Mr B[u] to Eden[b]——
Glasgow
Hamilton
Falls of the Clyde
Lanark
Carnwath
Edinburgh

---

[1] This person, mentioned again on p. 72, was probably Hector MacDonald Buchanan, the Laird of Ross Priory. See facsimile letter in George S. Hellman, *Washington Irving, Esquire,* opposite p. 100.

[II, 24] rivers celebrated by Burns[1]
Doon—Lugar—Ayr—Nith   Cluden
favorite walks on the banks of the Nith or the
    Cluden—
particularly near ruins of Lincluden abbey—
Athol house—Tilt—Bruar water
Burns rapture on the banks of the Tilt—[2]

[II, 26] Glasgow
         Dumbarton ⎫
         Mr Buchanans ⎬
         Lochlomond ⎭
         Loch Catrine
         Callander
         Lochearnhead
         Killin
         Taymouth
         Blair
         Dunkeld

[1] Irving had in mind presumably such poems as: *Sweet Are the Banks o' Doon, The Brigs of Ayr, The Banks o' Doon, Behind Yon Hills Where Lugar Flows, The Banks of Nith, The Humble Petition of Bruar Water*. See also *To William Simpson of Ochiltree,* Stanza VIII:

> Ramsay an' famous Fergusson
> Gied Forth an' Tay a lift aboon;
> Yarrow an' Tweed, to monie a tune,
>   Owre Scotland rings;
> While Irwin, Lugar, Ayr, an' Doon
>   Naebody sings.

[2] Opposite this page (II, 25), is a full-page sketch of hills and towers. The caption of the picture is illegible.

Perth
Crieff
Dunblane

[II, 27]   Stirling
Linlithgow
Edinburgh
From Edin^h to Glasgow
Lanark
Falls of Clyde
Hamilton
Glasgow

[II, 29] 1817 Sept 7^{th1} leave Edinburgh
in chaise for Linlithgow—ride through low
rich scenery of Mid Lothian & west Lothian
—Leith water with pleasant banks. 10 mile
stone walk to Niddry castle—a square tower
walls of immense thickness—small burn winding round the foot of it—dungeon[2]

pleasant approach to Linlithgow—in a
road between two sloping banks. Old palace
& church on a knoll [?] with river winding
at its base

church   old woman who shows the steeple
—Never saw Bogles[3]

---

[1] For this date and others, see itinerary of Irving's
tour in Scotland, Introduction, pp. 10-12.
[2] Irving has drawn a small ground plan of the castle.
[3] Hobgoblins.

Palace—woman who shows it Bowie [?]
family been there 200 years—

Loch—green banks sweeping into [?] it.
cock crowing

[II, 30] Linlithgow Palace stands on a
green knoll with a beautiful lake before it.
Rich tint of the stone—large court. Over the
windows are the rose & thistle surmounted by
the cross [?]. Cock crowing from one of the
windows makes the court resound—

 ˙ Woman that shews it of the name of Bowie
[?]—Has the hereditary privilege of shewing the castle & fishing the lake & makes col-
lard[1] [*sic*] eels which are sent all over the
world. Her ancestors have been in the service
of the castle for 200 years. Her mother saw
the Pretender when he was only 8 years of
age & took him by the coat—he was a pretty
gentleman

—Room where Queen Mary was born—
Spacious though the ceiling must have been
low—fine long corridors—large council room
—Dining room. private chapel

[II, 31]—Kitchen like a cavern, immense
arched fire places

[II, 33] Linlithgow church.

Old Tibbie who shews the steeple & says

---

[1] Boned, or rolled up.

she rings the Bells. 79 years old—Says she
never saw a bogle—

Mrs Bowie [?] accuses old Tibbie of telling untruths—says she gets the idle boys
(blacks) of the town of an evening & gives
them a cup of coffee & bannock[1] & gets them
to ring the bells

[II, 34] Falkirk. Sunday evening—Town
in something of a stir from the arrival of
country people from different parts to attend
a Cattle Fair.

A dull, dismal looking place though the
misty weather may give a gloom to it. The
scenery around is fine, particularly the castle
but the gloomy weather prevents its being
seen to advantage—

[II, 35] Monday morning 8. Leave Falkirk about nine, on foot for Stirling. Pass
by Carron works[2]—no admittance—beautiful
scenery in the neighborhood of the works—
mist clears off & the sun comes out bright &
warm. Falkirk cattle fair on a moor   High-
landers in plaids—See but one or two in
kilts. small black cattle. Sheep with black
faces & legs. The road[s?] are full of droves

---

[1] A cake of coarse meal baked on a griddle or hot
stone.

[2] Part of the iron industry of Falkirk.

of cattle pouring along towards Falkirk picturesque figures of herdsmen with highland
blue bonnets—plaids wrapped round them &
staff under the arm. Shepherd dogs following—small men of hardy sunburnt counte-
nances—Country very rich & well cultivated
with the alloa mountains in the distance

The approach to Falkirk is uncommonly
beautiful—The Town & Castle rising out of
a rich valley, "Gray Falkirk."

[II, 36] At the turnpike gate a little short
of Stirling we get a girl to shew us the field
of Bannock Burn—an old woman points to
us Gillies Hill & says its there the soldiers
came—what soldiers I asked—The Scots—
our auld decrepit men & women—

We see the stone where the Bruces stand-
ard was planted—called the Kings Stone—
fine view of Stirling from this place.[1]

[II, 39] Falkirk fair on the muir—Droves
of small highland black cattle. Little tough
highlander bustling & bawling in welsh—men
with plaid swung round their shoulders. Dog
—as fine in years [?] as ever ran the braes[2]

[1] The next page (II, 37) bears a sketch, apparently of
persons sitting in the shade of trees. This may be an illus-
tration for a passage in the *Excursion to Runcorn*. See
p. 78.
[2] Small hills, or the slopes of small hills.

—handsome clean limbed tall young peasant light hair sun burnt ruddy cheek—blue animated eye—firm tread[1]

[II, 42] Stirling castle evening—castle turned into Barracks &c. The guard room[2] where Ellen was rec[d] is beside the portal Door opening into the court—

view from Stirling castle at Sunset—clouds & mist shrouding some part of the prospect. splendid effect of sun darting her rays into the mist—

—Alloa mountains. nearer one of an inky hue—others lighter—sun seen gleaming on a mountain at a distance. Singular windings of the forth called the links of forth because like a chain—

Grotesque figures on the castle.

Visit the Gaol where the carvings are which were taken from Stirling castle—Gaolar [*sic*]—a large ruddy robust man full of talk & jokes—shews old scottish measures—& old invalid soldier who [II, 43] points out the house where George Buchanan[3] lived—the

---

[1] On II, 40, is a drawing called "Stirling From Bannock Burn."

[2] See "The Lady of the Lake," Canto Sixth, Stanzas 1-10.

[3] George Buchanan (1506-1582), scholar and historian, author of *Rerum Scoticarum Historia* (1582), lived at Stirling castle as tutor to James VI from 1570 to 1578.

Duke of Argyles[1] barn now an hospital—The Earl of Mars[2] projected residence—never finished—

Morning 9th—brilliant clear day—valley of the forth. mist rising from it. Smoke from cottages. Forth gleaming like silver [II, 44] from Stirling Castle looking up towards NWest. Long lines of mountains in the distance. fertile valley hamlets—lines of cottages—road intersecting it—forth winding thro. See horsemen traversing the road—the noise of waggons rattling away below—feeble shouts of children—sun here & then lost—then gleaming again—Castle high above me on crags—crows and choughs wheeling round it—cool morning breeze—smoke wreathing up from thatchd cottages—cocks crowing —twittering of birds—reapers in distant field mostly women—Old men taking their morning walk round the castle rock

Mountain purplish brown with heath *north* [?] part dusky greenish grey—Dark green patches of Pine wood

[II, 45] Tower of Cambus Kenneth Abbey

Leave Stirling in coach for Perth—find on

---

[1] The family of the Campbells.
[2] The family of the Erskines.

top of coach Mr Dent of Worcester—beautiful ride up the valley—with Stirling at a
distance—rock of Stirling completely cover-
ing the town—Craig—Forth at distance on
our left—country bare and heathy—fine purple tint of the mountain Pass thro Dunblane
—not a handsome woman in it. Guard of
coach says he has made diligent inquiry &
believes the story of Jessy[1] entirely a fiction
—fine old church in ruins—

The latter part of the ride within 10 miles
of Perth grows beautiful. Ride along Allan
water—See Invermay on our right

[II, 46] Perth—are shewn the house by a
fellow passenger. Mr Robinson[2] of Glasgow.
Steamboat proprietor—a Dandy Dinmont
character—

Tay a limpid beautiful stream—fine
Bridge—

[II, 47] Kinnoul craigs [?] famous boul-
ders

[?] fine [?] site [?] of Beltis [?] or May
Day

retreat of Wallace[3]

---

[1] Probably an allusion to the song, *Jessie, the Flower
o' Dunblane.* See p. 66, and footnote 2.

[2] Compare p. 129.

[3] These three entries are scribbled in the margin and
are nearly illegible.

Morning. Wednesday—10ᵗʰ Walk up to
craig of Kinnoul—from side of the hill have
a fine view of perth and the adjacent country
—great valley with the Tay winding thro—
Palace of Scone on left—Grampian hills in
distance coverd with mist—twittering of
birds—smoke rising from cottage chimneys—
peasant girls with milk, thread [?] &c going
to the fair—tall pretty girl with milk pails
singing a Scotch song

Rob Roy[1]

[II, 48] The prospect from the craig of
Kinnoul is one of the noblest I ever beheld
You are placed on the edge of an impending
precipice of some hundred feet that forms
part of a ridge of crags—butting over a
beautiful & fertile vale—the Tay winds below you and at a distance makes a grand
sweep with the hills of Fife shire beyond

1 Mentioned again on p. 64. Scott's novel did not
appear until the next year (1818), but Irving knew from
G. C. Verplanck, and perhaps from Scott himself, that
the book was in preparation: "I find it is pretty generally believed that Scott is the author of those novels,
and Verplanck tells me he [Scott] is now travelling
about, collecting materials for Rob Roy." Letter to
Peter Irving, London, August 19, 1817, *Life and Letters
of Washington Irving,* I, 373-375. See *ibid.,* I, 378-384:
". . . I shall be able to trace Scott in his Rob Roy
scenery."

picturesque hights [*sic*] with telegraphs[1]—
river gleams like a broad sheet of silver—with
the sun beams

Flight of crows far below me—

Road passes below the craig & I hear the
noise of a cart tho the cart & horse are extremely diminished by the hight—rush of the
wind through the trees of the cliff—whistles
thro the grass that grows on the brow of the
precipice—I hear the whooping of children
but cannot perceive them.

[II, 49] Front of crags beautifully tinted
—golden or rather rusty tints—grey greenish &c.—hear voices and songs of peasants
from the valley but cannot see the men

French Depot—Inches[2] east end of the
town—fine lawns with Tay running by them
—

Old abbey in ruins in perth

Leave perth in gig—here at 8 friday & a
boy perched up behind—boys name Robert

Horses name Blaze—trots behind & walks
before. great expense of the lash. pass some
fine heath—read macbeth—As the road ap-

[1] Obviously not the electric telegraph. This word was
in common use in France and England before 1800. See
New English Dictionary.

[2] Small islands, or low lands near a river.

proaches Dunkeld it becomes extremely
grand—Tay wind[g] thro romantic scenery—

Birnam wood—collect some oak leaves—
man at the gate tells us about Macbeth

[II, 83] Old Scot. had herded for many
years on the grampian hills—Saw Norvals[1]
grave there—& Macbeths castle [?]—Present Laird o' Dunsinane is as himmil a mon
as ever you saw in your life—he would talk
wi you—just like an auld wife an for a that
he had an awfu knowledge o' the law.[2]

[II, 50] Fine view of Dunkeld from the
Hill—tower of the Church appearing over
the Duke of Athols ground[3]—

—country round richly wooded mountains
clothed with trees—pretty country girl with
fine eyes—country girls often pretty until 14
or 15 when excessive work in the fields makes
them coarse & hard favour[d]—

[1] Irving refers several times to Young Norval, the
hero of John Home's play, *Douglas* (1756, 1757).~Com-
pare *Notes while preparing Sketch Book &c.*, p. 61; and
in this volume p. 24.

[2] The last phrase of the note, "awfu knowledge o' the
law," occurs in the other volume of the two notebooks,
and is used with changes in "Abbotsford," *The Crayon
Miscellany*. See p. 24 in the present volume.

[3] The estates of the Murrays. The most distinguished
members of the family were: John Murray, second Earl
and first Marquis of Atholl (1635?-1703); John Murray,
second Marquis and first Duke of Atholl (1659-1724);
John Murray, third Duke of Atholl (1729-1774).

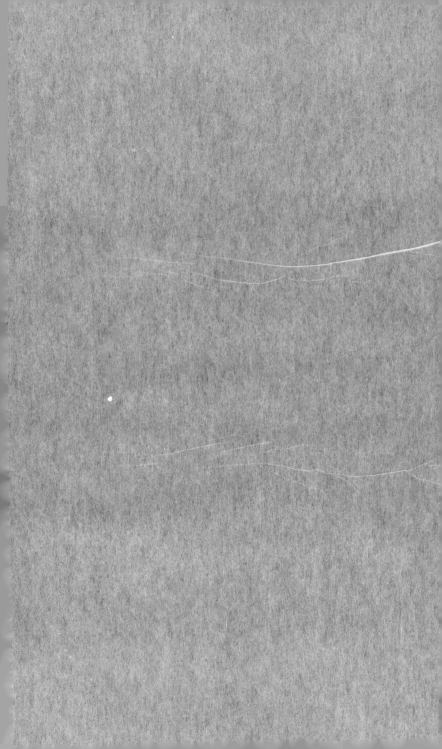

*A fine view of Dunkeld from
the hill - tower of the church appears
on the Duke of Athol's grounds -
- country round richly wooded
mountains clothed with trees -
pretty country girl with fine eyes -
country girls often pretty. until 13 or 15
when exposure work in the fields make
them coarse & hard-favoured.*

BISHOP'S TOMB IN DUNKELD CHURCH

[II, 51] Dunkeld church—Huge columns & arches—Badenochs[1] mutilated statue & tomb[2]—crows cawing—clock from old town strikes three—Ivy over the wall—old sextons annuities buried him grey colors of the stone.

[II, 52] Story of Grocer at perth that the Earl of Dunsinane employed 30 men to dig in ruins of Macbeths castle—they found bones—but the people were so superstitious that they fancied they saw ghosts &c and would not work.

[II, 53] Dunkeld—from the Bridge. 5 O'Clock Broken clouds. rich gleams of Sunshine falling on mountains & on the Stream—Old cathedral town—gray—part of cathedral overrun with ivy—smoke curling up from various parts of the town—draws a haze like gauze over the green of the mountains—Gay confusion of mountain tree[s?] —stream &c.—Broad river—rippling stream —shingle beach—grey stones—clothes spread to bleach on the shore. children watching the clothes—fire made under a garden

[1] Alexander Stuart, Earl of Buchan and Lord of Badenoch (1343?-1405?), son of Robert II of Scotland, and known as "The Wolf of Badenoch."

[2] On the opposite page (II, 50) Irving has drawn a sketch, "Bishop's Tomb."

wall to boil clothes—groups of villagers some with plaids—Sun falling upon a green table of land—and gleaming green beneath the trees—

Clouds—Soft clear colors—rich silver opening thro which the sun gleams Dark reflections of the mountains on the water— but wherever there[1] [II, 55] is a ripple in the water it catches a sunbeam & glistens amid surrounding gloom

Niel Gows[2] favorite seat under an immense oak—twilight—bank of the Tay—dark flow of the water—salmon leaping—hooting of the owl—Bell tolling the hour at a distance & echoed among the mountains—whistle of boy among the trees—tread of horse at distance—lowing of cattle sounding thro mountains—noise of cart in woods & gossiping of peasants—

Contrast between quiet flow of the broad deep Tay & the brawling of the shallow Brunn [Braan?]

Bridge 30 or 40 feet high two officers

[1] At this point (II, 54) occurs a full-page sketch, "Craig Kinnoul."

[2] Niel Gow (1727-1807), a violinist and composer of music, and popular in English and Scottish society. Irving may possibly refer to Gow's son (d. 1823), of the same name, the composer of *Bonnie Prince Charlie*.

riding at full speed could not turn quick
enough one gave his horse the [II, 57] rein
& sprang over into the stream without injury
—the other was injured against the parapet
—Prestons[1] story of his ride—determined to
cross pine creek by a certain time—landlord
told him that if floods were up he would be
swept away against a rock round which the
flood boiled & foamed. As he rode thro the
pine woods along precipice fringed with trees
had now & then a glimpse of gulph of the
valley with mist steaming up it & occasionally
wrapping him in cloud—heard the torrent
roaring—when he came to it found water
over the ford—pulled off coat & boots & tied
them behind the saddle—Horse swam with
his breast up the stream & got over safe.

Borders of South Carolina—in the war
there were many Scotch—anecdotes similar
to border history—one scot who was wounded
dreadfully told surgeon never mind me I
shall be in heaven or h——[2] in half an hour
but there is a poor fellow lost his leg tend to
him [II, 58] After surgeon had dressed the

[1] William C. Preston, of South Carolina, Irving's
traveling companion. See Introduction, pp. 13, 14. Although these anecdotes are concerned with America, they
were apparently told to Irving by Preston during the
tour; and they are, therefore, set down here.

[2] Irving's dash.

wounds of the others he returned to this man & found him yet alive—cured him—& the officers of the reg^t were so pleased with his magnanimous conduct that they subscribed & made him an annuity—

Sept 11   Thursday—left Dunkeld at ½ past six & rode to Balnaguard.—10 miles— fine ride along the Tay valley with frequent views of the river—pass some fine plantations and the country generally better worked than I had expected. Misty morning—but very mild & pleasant—Sun gleams out among the mountains.

Balnaguard a mere collection of miserable hovels—huts of stone & clay with roofs thatched of straw & heather—some have small inclosures in which a scanty stock of cabbages are raised—some few apologies for windows stopped up with rags boards &c Small [II, 59] streams wandering thro the village—stone bridge of rude workmanship thrown over it near the Inn—

Public house dirty—but breakfast abundant—

6 miles to Aberfeldy—on the way pass the small castle on left of Gaunther [?] turrets at corners—girl sewing by the side of the road singing scotch air.

—at Aberfeldy visit the falls of Moness—
one falls called the falls of the Birks of Aberfeldy where Burns wrote his song[1]—

Thence 7 miles to Taymouth—noble seat
of Marquis of Breadalbane in castellated
form [II, 61] Kenmore—beautiful view
Loch Tay from the road—row to little island—ruins of convent built in time of Alex
I. Kenmore church & village—with sunshine
on it—bridge—lake calm—boat on the beach
of the Island—sunbeams on distant heathery
mountains—Lowing of cattle from side of
mountain

Large Lime trees round the convent

Trout leaping in the lake

Towers from Bradalbane Castle

Walk after dusk in the grounds of Marquis of Breadalbane—singular cry of a bird
high in the air which I could not see—sound
of Kenmore clock—fine highland boy riding
boldly like a soldier—village children running afraid [II, 62] of ghosts—

Friday—leave at 7 oclock—beautiful
warm morning sun breaking beautifuly
[*sic*] thro clouds—picturesque views of Ken-

---

[1] *The Birks of Aberfeldie*, written by Burns as he
stood near the falls of Moness. Irving quotes the fifth
stanza of this poem in *Notes while preparing Sketch
Book &c.* See p. 67.

more from various parts of the Lake Little
island of the convent—

Old hovels of stone & rubbish—Thatchd,
coverd with moss—grass under—fir grove—
Mountain ash hangs over them its red tassels

Loch Tay—Darkened by passing clouds—
Kenmore church in the shade—but beyond—
the heathy mountains down the course of the
Tay are in sunshine. [II, 63] so from the
gloom of adversity look out on the prosperity
of the world—

As we go up the Loch Tay it seems as if
we were riding into regions of darkness—
mountains ahead all overshadowed by clouds
& tops coverd with mist—behind is all sunshine

Lion Mountain—seen away up a vast
mountain Depth [?] like a lion in his Den.
top shrouded—Ben lui coverd with mist

Mountains begin to look thin & sterile—
Scarred with gullies

Mountaineer—who boasted of his mountains—Ben Lui &c

Clouds   thicker—rain—fine   rainbow—
mountain under it mottled with sunshine—
above the mountain appearing darkly thro
mist—

[II, 64] Killin—wild brook breaking its way thro the village—

Old castle & Chapel of L Breadalbane. Old game keeper & his Staff—his story of Mans head struck off that said Kirk Kirk Kirk

woman begging—this is a bonny country Sir—A bonny place between the Knowes[1]—a bonny chapel for Ld Bradalbn—when hes gone been buried when hell [he'll] be dead—mony thanks sir & wish you safe home till your ain country

[II, 65] road from Killin to Loch Earne Road passes through glen with stream rolling thro—this turns up a mountain & thro a wild rocky glen—Druidical stones heavy rain and wind in the glen—arrive at Loch Earne 8 miles—weather holds up & lake looks wild—

Stream rumbling sound—flies playing idly over it

[II, 69] Perth—Sept—10th 1817.

I lett a Gig and Horse to Mr Irving at eight Shillings per day. The Boy that accompanys the gig to be found. If the gig is relinquished at Callander Mr Irving is to pay twelve Shillings for the expenses of the Gig back to Perth. If there is any detention from

[1] Knolls.

defect of Horse or gig, Mr I to pay nothing
for the time taken up by such detention.

Jas K Norning [?]¹

[I, 124] Saturday. Sept 13²—Lochearne
Head glorious sunrise—S rising at lower end
of the lake full in view of our chamber window

Leave Lochearne head 7 oclock ride by
mountain pass see the Braes of Balquhidder
on our left—grand mountain glen—small
lake of Lubnaig surrounded by grand mountains—Ben Ledi, at lower end—silver sheet
of water. road passes along its banks—pass
picturesque height on which the chapel of Sᵗ
Bride used to stand—vide Scotts Lady of the
lake³—ride along the Teith—Ben Ledi on
our left—thro the pass of Lennie [Leny]—
waterfalls bridge &c came to Callander—
Country opens—Teith flows past Callander.

¹ Written on a separate page in the notebook, this
entry was probably recorded before the notations immediately preceding it. Except the signature the handwriting appears to be Irving's.
² The narrative now continues in the larger notebook.
On I, 125, is a faint sketch of Ben Ledi.
³ Throughout his tour Irving was deeply interested in
places associated with Scott's fiction and poetry:

When rose Benledi's ridge in air; . . ."
The Complete Poetical Works of Sir Walter Scott,
"The Lady of the Lake," Canto First, line 105.

A blithsome rout that morning-tide
Had sought the chapel of Saint Bride. . . ."
Ibid., Canto Third, lines 478, 479.

Breakfast here after breakfast ride by ford
of Coilantogle &c & to Stewarts where we have
home and go thro Trossachs to Loch Katrine
—beautiful day—ramble about the Lake visit
the —— &c and return to Stewarts where we
pass the night

[I, 122] Approach to Trossachs—beautiful view of Loch Achray from opening between two knolls—Knolls with birch interval
coverd with heath[1]

Schehallion

[I, 123] Numerous echoes on lake Katrine
opposite BenVenue—

Stewart—sturdy highlander. Old Beggar
in chimney corner to whom Stewart gives a
bed because he said he would fight for prince
charles if necessary—

On asking Stewart if we could be accom-
modated—Ow, ay, ai can gie ye plenty to
eat and a stretch out—some time or other—
told him we were easy satisfied   oh if your
travellers Im no feard—but sometimes these
society [?] southern folk are hard to please.
told him we were americans—oh he never
found an American yet that could not be
content with any thing—

[1] This jotting was evidently added later by Irving as
an insertion. It is so marked by lines in the manuscript.

Large fine place   Old beggar with plaid
—gray hair & 79

Old Beggar & Stewart also affirm that
Bonaparte is a son of Roy Stewart who ac-
companied prince charles—left his country
[I, 122] and changed his name—thinks the
Stewarts will yet return—

Bedroom—earth floor—two Beds or re-
cesses with curtains—Large clock—wooden
corner cupboard two queer pictures by some
tyro—of a highlander & lass

Book of stories of Loch Katrine with
Buchanan of Baltimore[1] name in—Stewart—
reddish short curly hair—rather thin on top
—stout middle aged man roman nose

[I, 121] Large fine place—bench and
chairs in corner   Dogs &c
Sept 14—

Sunday Morning—fine summer weather—
joined by two young men Germans & two
large Scotsmen—discharge the gig & take
boat for head of Loch catrine   Bugle sound

---

[1] Possibly Franklin Buchanan (1800-1874), who began
his career in the American navy as a midshipman in
1815. It is more likely that Irving refers to George
Buchanan (1698?-1750), physician and jurist. He was
born in Scotland, but aided in founding the city of Baltimore. Or he alludes to George Buchanan (1763-1808),
physician and author, and one of the city magistrates of
Baltimore.

among the hills—land at Cauldburn—grand
solitary glen between Loch Katrine & Loch
Lomond—about half way from high part of
the road see loch Katrine—with summit of
BenLedi   Ben Venue &c—on other hand
dark mountains of Loch Lomond 3 Bens—
Little loch of[1] [I, 120] Inversnaid fort—on
a rising ground—Delta formed by two
brooks Grand view of Benvorlich—Gate way
into large loch & hills. large holes in walls.
old swivel on angle flanking towers at two
corners—across to it from Loch Lomond a
narrow foot bridge over a burn—commanded
by a knoll with rocks—path winds up the hill.
Soldiers burying place on a knoll.

Bugle summons to castle of Inversnaid
women about the castle—Old woman looking
thro the window

party Mr Sheriff a Scot—two Mr Grants
—a young German

[I, 118] Approach to Ben Lomond—road
winding down a hight on which sun shines—
opposite mountain is dark purple

Huge mountains—dark purple black
shadows over the water—little green inter-

---

[1] Irving did not finish the phrase. The page ends with
a sketch of mountains, unnamed, extending over upon
the opposite page (I, 121). At the top of this page is a
drawing of Ben Nevis and Ben Vorlich.

vale with cottage as if reposing in the giant bosom
arms[1] [*sic*] of the mountain. Gigantic embraces

Soft rich green turf slopes down the mountain—summer house of Stewart on left

Mill of Inversnaid[2]—large fine place. Old smoaky books—some latin—pretty little orphan girl—blue eyes & yellow hair—tends the Kyl [?][3]

Story of Hermit & officers negro hunt [?].

water fall near the mill—water of Inversnayd—take boat at the mill & visit Rob Roys cave—a cleft among rocks—sometimes he hid 80 men—the cave at a picturesque point of rocks—Ash—lichens &c

[I, 114] From Rob Roys cave we are rowed to Tarbet—our Boatman as smuggler

[1] Such arrangements of words are frequent in the notebooks and hint at Irving's experiments in writing. Compare in this volume, pp. 100, 118.

[2] Opposite (I, 119), is a dim sketch, perhaps of the mill. The next three pages (I, 117, 116, 115) bear sketches. The first two pages present a drawing of a castle, and of mountains, inscribed "———— heart of perthshire." What appears to be Rob Roy's cave is at the right in the foreground. The other drawing shows the mountains "opposite Rob Roys cave," and records the colors of the hills: "green," "touches of green," "dk purple."

[3] The word is nearly illegible, but may be the Scottish dialect word for "cows" or "kine."

Inn at Tarbet good—beautifully situated
—evening walk to Loch Long—

Sept 15 Monday morning—leave Tarbet
at ½ past 8—across the lake. walk to tip of
Loch Lomond—MacIntyre our guide—has
stories of Rob Roy &c —descend the mountain to[1]

reembark in boat to Luss—from Luss take
boat to head of Leven. Fair of cattle—walk
down Leven to Dumbarton

Our Boatmen from Luss were McLelland a
shoemaker & McFarlane a weaver. The latter
had an intelligent countenance—seemed well
informed for a man in his situation—had
read the hist. of Scotland & was authentic as
to dates—when McLelland pretended to speak
he said hoot mon yed better let these tales be
—ye dinna ken the right of em—

Two drunken fellows staggering from the
fair singing a pastoral of Burns

of all the Airts the wind can blow &c[2]

[I, 113] near Tarbet—

[1] Irving's blank.
[2] The song Burns composed for his wife during their
honeymoon:

> Of a' the airts the wind can blaw
> I dearly like the west,
> For there the bonie lassie lives,
> The lassie I lo'e best.
> . . .

Mountain stream falling down black rocks Sun shining on it makes it like a shower of diamonds—trees hanging over it—Holly with glossy leaf & scarlet berry—Oak—weeping birch with tender leaf—Mountain ash light & graceful—Ivy running up trees— moss—fern &c

The Scots villages are dirty and mere collections of hovels, but the people seem curious, communicative & social.

In our voyage from Luss pass in sight of[1] the burying place of the MacGregors—also Lenox castle in ruins—

[I, 112] Luss peasant had killed an adder unco [?] but is frightsome [?] said a pretty blue eyed woman

unco—but its a bonnie beast said an old woman called nannie

Story told by Sheriff of a young man a weaver of Paisley who composed three or four beautiful songs Jessie o Dunblane—dreamy [?] writer [?]—he was of a melancholy turn & drowned himself—his name was Tannihill [Tannahill][2]

[1] Irving leaves a blank space. For his other allusions to the MacGregors, Rob Roy's clan, see p. 134.
[2] Robert Tannahill (1774-1810), a writer of Scottish songs, who was brought up as a silk-weaver in Paisley. His poems were published in 1807. Among his famous

Dumbarton castle—situated on a conical rock rising romantically from the banks of the Clyde and connected to the mainland by a low peninsula—

Sept 16—

Tuesday morning—waiting for steam boat —seated on a rock at the foot of Dumbarton castle—Hazy warm day—Sun just struggling thro the haze—tide low beach grey stone and swallows [?] coal smack floating lazily in—hear now & then the creaking of the yards—& hum of the [I, 111] boatmans song who is pacing his deck with folded arms —boat at a point of rocks on which was my companion Preston—Sherif[1] & young ger-

songs were *Braes o' Gleniffer* and *Jessie, the Flower o' Dunblane.* The first of the three verses of this song follows:

> The sun has gane down o'er the lofty Benlomond,
> And left the red clouds to preside o'er the scene,
> While lanely I stray in the calm simmer gloamin',
>   To muse on sweet Jessie, the flow'r o' Dumblane.
> How sweet is the brier, wi' its saft faulding blossom,
> And sweet is the birk, wi' its mantle o' green;
>   Yet sweeter an' fairer, and dear to this bosom,
> Is lovely young Jessie the flow'r o' Dumblane,
> Is lovely young Jessie, the flow'r o' Dumblane.

See song, set to music by R. A. Smith, in *Music Miscellany,* n.p., n.d., IV, 32. The name is spelled in two ways: "Dunblane" or "Dumblane." Compare Irving's allusions to this song on pp. 49, 126. See also *The Works of Robert Tannahill,* . . . London, 1848, pp. 2, 3.

[1] Irving spells the name of this acquaintance in different ways.

man—birds singing from the rocks over my head. hum of large flies about me—tokens of happiness [?] of Summer—Dumbarton across the narrow bay that separates it from the castle—smoke from glass houses.

N B. recollect the night spent on old roman rock in highlands.

Take steamboat for Glasgow   view down Clyde Dunglass castle in middle ground. Dumbarton rock & castle in the Distance

[I, 108] Sept. 17. 7 oclock. coach to Ayr— pass thro poor moorish country. by Kingswell

a few miles (about 2) from Glasgow pass Langsyde [Langside] house where the forces of Mary were defeated—to our left we saw the knoll from which she saw the battle—

About Kilmarnock & down to Ayr the country is soft & fertile—pass the stream of Irvine—where Wallace killed two or three of the English who disturbed him when fishing

put up at Kings arms' at Ayr—go to Galloway church   Doon river &c—

In the evening the theatre   Edinburgh company—morning return to Glasgow—intelligent guard—from Glasgow take mail coach to Hamilton—pass Bothwell Bridge— see Bothwell tower on banks of the Clyde—

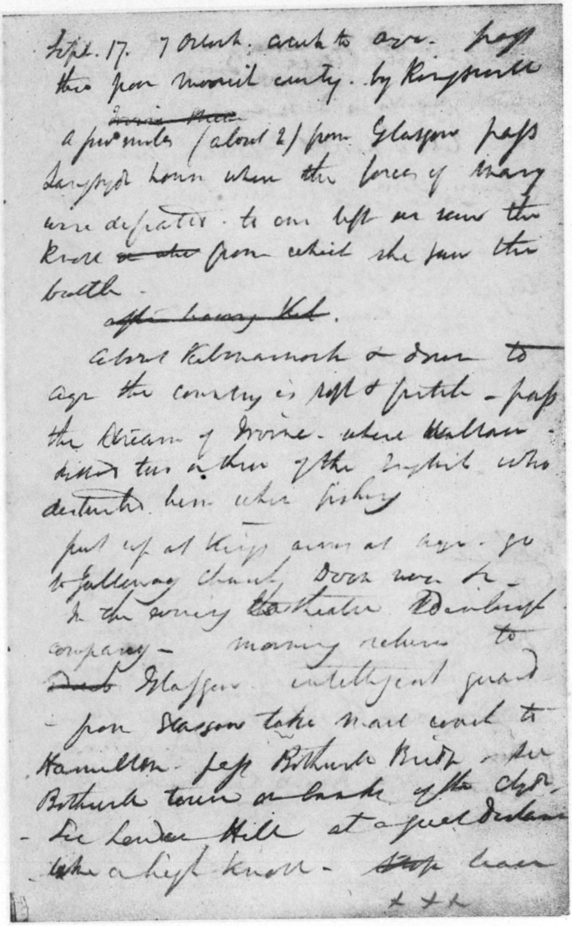

IRVING'S VISIT TO AYR

See London Hill at a great distance like a high Knoll—Leave[1]

[I, 107] Ayr Wallace's Tower—story told of it by old man in neighborhood who held a property chartered from him—fairy stories —Wallace head—& foot

Story of Wallace burning the Barns of Ayr and retreating to neighbouring hill from whence he said the Barns of Ayr burn weel & it is called Burnweel to this day

Kirk Alloway on a mound   Doon running at a short distance—Mason John Tennant at work repairing it for a school house—near the gate the grave of Burns father[2]

[I, 106] Douglas Graeme—o'Shanter— a farm Kirk Oswald Old man in alloway [?] & a evil [?] boy he was—uncle Jemmy [?] some kind a wee bit touch [?] upon him & a niece living with him I dinna mind what. her uncle Jemmy a cousin of mine just. Jemmy married upon a —— in May time [?][3]

Alloway church-yard lolling on grass by

[1] This paragraph, seemingly out of order, is recorded in the sequence of the passages in the notebook.

[2] Following these notes, (I, 104), is the most graceful drawing in the two volumes, the Brig of Doon. On I, 102, is a sketch of hills. Irving has again noted the colors of the landscape.

[3] This passage is nearly illegible.

church door—Stone mason telling stories of
Burns Soft mild day.

Sons of shanter failed—one—Pitton [?]
owns the farm.

Mason had drank with Burns

[I, 26] Dungeon Tower at Ayr[1]—Twilight—Guards in high helmets with long
horsehair crests slowly pacing backwards &

[1] Irving's tour of Scotland with William C. Preston
began Sunday, September 7, and ended Friday, September 19. He arrived in Ayr on the evening of Wednesday,
September 17. The entry is out of regular sequence in
the notebooks. For a detailed itinerary see pp. 10-12.

The pilgrimage to Ayr has interest as a suggestion of
the influence of Burns upon Irving during this period.
In the *Notes while preparing Sketch Book &c.,* he quotes
from Burns (p. 67). There are allusions to Burns in
Irving's published works, but few references, save these,
to Burns in the letters and journals. The influence, compared, for example, to that of Spanish writers, seems to
have been transient. These notes, however, Irving used
in writing "Abbotsford":

"Let me step forward in time, and mention how sen-
sible I was to the power of these simple airs, in a visit
which I made to Ayr, the birthplace of Robert Burns. I
passed a whole morning about 'the banks and braes of
bonnie Doon,' with his tender little love-verses running
in my head. I found a poor Scotch carpenter at work
among the ruins of Kirk Alloway, which was to be converted into a school-house. Finding the purpose of my
visit, he left his work, sat down with me on a grassy
grave, close by where Burns' father was buried, and
talked of the poet, whom he had known personally. He
said his songs were familiar to the poorest and most
illiterate of the country folk, '*and it seemed to him as if
the country had grown more beautiful since Burns had
written his bonnie little songs about it.*'" *The Crayon
Miscellany,* pp. 257, 258.

forwards on a kind of terrace in front. Tower Dark & massive—large arched door way thro which is seen a murky light. Soldier going up the broad flight of steps—lazily with military garment thrown across his Musket

Twilight at foot of old Tower called the castle of Forth—Sky clear & mellow over head—a smoky horizon—distant sound of the bugle notes of the bagpipe—distant shrill shouts of children at play—Tower of Brown stone stands lonely on a common—bark of dog—half moon rising—enlarged by smoky horizon one side of the tower with a [I, 27] grand sunset at Ayr—Bridges &c fort—like a Claude Lorraine evening

Mellow dubious light from the last lingering of day the other side dark

[I, 101] the coach at Kirkmoor hill—take a horse & cart for Lanark where we find it difficult to get beds—lodged at John Muirs [?] Friday—Visit Cartland Crags. Wallaces Cave small cave where he was said to be concealed—grey rocks—Birch—weeping birch—ash—return to breakfast & then visit arms [?] manufactory—children at play at school—have evening amusem^t [?] 700 workmen 2500 people—eating houses &c &c—visit falls of Clyde. Coralinns [Cora Linns] & upper falls—difficulty of procuring a chaise at Lanark—Kindness of Mrs Jean Pent [?] hostess—pretty woman

Arrive in Edinburgh ½ past 8 ocl[1]—after a fine ride across a heath with rich melting horizon—and Highlands in the Distance

[I, 100] Saturday 21—Dine at Jeffreys[2] —company Mr Hector McDonald [*sic*] Buchanan[3] Mr Rutherford Mr Thomson— &c—

Sunday 22   Leave Edinburgh[4] in mail for Selkirk—

[1] This was Friday, September 19. See letter to Peter Irving, dated Edinburgh, September 20, 1817, in which he says, "I arrived here late last evening . . ." *Life and Letters of Washington Irving*, I, 384.

[2] Compare: "I dined yesterday with Jeffrey, and found a very agreeable party of Edinburgh gentlemen there; I cannot but repeat how much I feel obliged to Jeffrey for his particular attentions, and the very friendly manner in which he has deported towards me." Letter to Peter Irving, Edinburgh, Sunday, September 22, 1817, *ibid.*, I, 386. For facts concerning this date see Introduction, p. 12, footnote 1.

[3] Compare p. 41.

[4] On the following day Irving paid Scott a farewell visit, but found him absent. *Ibid.*, I, 387. The rough draft of his farewell letter to Scott is printed in *Notes while preparing Sketch Book &c.*, pp. 84, 85.

Brig of Doon

BRIG O' DOON AT AYR

II.

EXCURSION TO RUNCORN

EXCURSION TO RUNCORN[1]

JUNE 23. Preston. P.[2] & myself. By steam boat which leaves Liverpool ½ past 3 oclock—On board the Boat was a little stunted fellow 19 years old who played on the pandean pipes & beat the tambourine—and occasionally sang & acted. Dance of clowns or rather country Butchers—

weather uncommonly sultry—arrive at Runcorn 6 oclock—

Stroll to the ruins of Halton Castle & lodge at the inn established in the castle—Magnificent view from the ruins which stand on a high insulated hill—& command a prospect on all sides of a rich extent of country with the Mersey winding through it. Seat of Sir Rob[t] Brooke[3] in the neighbourhood—

Ruins of the old castle over run with Ivy

[1] This journey with William C. Preston to the little river-port sixteen miles from Liverpool was made soon after Preston's arrival in England, in June, 1817.

[2] Probably Irving's brother, Peter. See *Life and Letters of Washington Irving, passim.*

[3] On p. 79 Irving speaks of Sir Richard Brooke. "Robert" is probably an error. It is possible that Irving refers to Richard Brooke (1791-1861) of Liverpool, the antiquary and philosopher.

—Old library in the vicinity of the castle under the care of the curate.

[II, 97] Askeys Inn—Halton Castle.

4?[1]

[II, 96] June 23 [*sic*] Rise at 5 oclock and walk around the height among the ruins of the castle. Bright sunny morning—Smoke curling up from the cottages of the hamlet at foot of the hill—country resounds with the song of various birds—Swallows skim around the hill & dart thro the arches of the old castle—cawing of rooks. Jocund crowing of village cocks—Lowing of herds—

The eastern horizon heavy with grey clouds—Grey mistiness of the landscape in that direction—long tracts of woodland of dark green—Smoke arising in a large mass from a manufactory several miles off. the smoke rises to a little height & then forms a long yellowish trail in the air hanging over the country for miles & partly blending with the clouds

Sounds of rural labour commence   Whistle of the plowman   The light cart preparing for market &c

[1] Corrected in ink, presumably in Irving's handwriting.

[II, 95] Prestons comparison of Steel traps &c amid lovely scenery to the toung [*sic*] of an adder under a rose bush.[1]

Theres vile human nature lurking among the beauties of innocent creation

retrospect
Comparison of week in town & in country

The retrospect of a week past in town is to look back upon a waste of comfortless existence—of sordid pursuits—jarring interests of feverish excitement of listlessness, & exhaustion. Our pleasures either trivial or vicious—turbulent passions—all the bad propensities of our nature aroused into action—

In the country our time passes innocently. Our excitements are those of the imagination —[II, 94] The current of thought flows purely & steadily—it may sometimes swell & expand, but never is whirled & hurried in turbid violence—Glorious reveries, sublime flights of imagination. Succeeded by quietude —not languor. A blessed repose of the mind

---

[1] Although Irving lived in England (1815-1832) during some of the fierce social and humanitarian controversies of the century, he is almost silent concerning these issues. A typical allusion occurs in "The Poor-Devil Author," *Tales of a Traveller*, p. 164.

—Every noble & gracious & gratifying [?] quality is brought out.[1]

[II, 93] Castle Inn kept by John Askey —His wife has 5 daughters by former husband—3 unmarried ones at home Martha Jane & Kate.

Jane amuses us by her philosophical reflections—discussion whether Beauty or wisdom is preferable. Jane resolute in favour of Wisdom.

5^2

June 24. [*sic*] Rise at 5 oclock & walk round the ruins of the castle.

at 8 leave the castle to embark in the steamboat—find that it has sailed—get a jaunting car and ride thro a Beautiful country & return to the castle—

Club of Poor Women assembled arrayed in their holliday [*sic*] clothes. A mutual relief club to assist each other in case of sickness— Groups of the [II, 92] neighbouring peasantry under the trees,[3] in a fine little grove on the slope of the hill

[1] This notation may have been one of Irving's random musings, and have been added later. Its position in the notebook indicates that it was written during the excursion to Runcorn.

[2] Corrected in ink, presumably by Irving.

[3] What appears to be a drawing of this scene occurs on II, 37.

Lady Brooke at the head of the club. They have a dinner at the castle inn. a great fete as perhaps the only time they taste meat in the course of the year.

Attempt to visit the library, but the Key is denied by curates wife—great indignation of Preston—Loll in one of the towers of the castle & read—In the afternoon visit the library—On his [?] Pannels [?] Old dusty books—

[II, 91] In the evening stroll in the grounds of Sir Richard Brooke—at night a Boxing match between two lads—probably of the mutual relief society

We were informed that most of the old women who composed the club did not taste meat from one end of the year to another—lived on Buttermilk potatoes &c   Some of them drank tea twice a day which with a little bread was their sustenance—Some of the poor lived on water porridge & potatoes two labouring men had died of consumption from hard work & poor living & two or three other were considered too much enfeebled ever to recover

III.

FRAGMENTS[1]

Notes on the West and South.
The Story of Rosalie.
*Personalia: Reading, Writing, and Miscellaneous
    Notes.*

[1] See Note on the Fragments, pp. 132-136.

HUNTER'S dress[1]—linsey trousers—Mocasins [*sic*] well greased—Hunting frock—of linen colour according to the season—green & yellow &c belted. live several weeks in the woods. farm also but poorly—Gentlemen make a party to hunt the bear—encamp for several days—live high—hangers on from around the country—

(Fishing parties—taylors of village &c) Sometimes turn out on alarm of a wolf in neighbourhood—whole country in a halloo— never catch the wolf but drive him from the country—

The hunters esteem killing the deer inferior sport—animal is shot down without knowing from whence the shot comes but to catch a great center [?] he (bear) in a laurel bush with dogs is rare sport—

[1] The following entries on hunting interrupt abruptly the account of the tours. The character of the writing suggests that they were recorded at another time, and their content hints that they were written after Irving's return to America, though there is the possibility that they were derived from reading. Compare the note on "Shenandoah," p. 85.

Hunter shot bear in belly   dog grappled with him—bear nearly killing him—hunter rushed in & stabbed bear in back of the shoulder. Buck sometimes makes sport by getting in the water where he touches [II, 73] bottom while dogs have to swim—cannot hurt them but knocks them under—sometimes cuts them with his feet

Young Y. sick confined to tent—hears the whooping of hunters   yelling of dogs a gun now & then roaring among the mountains—rude repast—Hunters Superstition: believe in their guns being charmed—in good omens, &c.   in dreams one if he dreamed of a dead-horn was sure of killing a deer & exerted himself so much as often to make the dream come true—borrow these superstitions from the Indians.

Shooting for Bears—have their choice according to the shot but Shot has hides & tallow—sometimes one gets all—old women of neighbourhood bring barrel of cider & ginger nuts—cider barrel put on two poles with a transverse piece—the whole drawn by a horse —whiskey—generally ends by a fight at night—no dancing—too rude for that amusement no girls attend

[II, 107] Shenandoah.[1]

Dutch settlers from Pennsylvania have supplanted the Virginians   Fertile grain country. with Blue ridge on one side & alleghany[2] on the other—180 miles long—Upper part of the valley called the Yankee county. County rich but property moderately distributed—No man over 100 or 150 000 $ most under 30,000—well cultivated.

Preston calls with a gent who had purchased land of Dutchman for 30,000$—in valley of Shenandoah—large well cultivated

[1] The next few entries on American life, like those which precede, may have been written during tours of the West and South made in 1832-1833. Irving left Tarrytown on August 4, 1832, for Saratoga Springs. His journey included Trenton Falls, Cincinnati, St. Louis, Independence (Missouri), Fort Gibson (Arkansas), New Orleans. In the mail stage he passed through Alabama, Georgia, South Carolina, North Carolina, and Virginia, stopping at Columbia to call on W. C. Preston, who is mentioned in these notes. He arrived in Washington by December 10, 1832. After leaving Washington he passed three weeks in Baltimore, and arrived at New York by April 1, 1833. In the latter part of April he again visited the South, stopping at Fredericksburg, Charlottesville, and was once more in New York before June 13, 1833. See *Life and Letters of Washington Irving,* III, 30-53. Material of the sort recorded here might well have been gathered on this journey, though no proof of this exists. It does not appear definitely in later writings, though there are seemingly echoes of these notes in *A Tour on the Prairies* (1835), and in *The Adventures of Captain Bonneville* . . . (1837).

[2] Irving's spelling of this name, as of many proper nouns, varies.

farm—Found farmer's wife seated in hall—
with shift & linsey woolsey petticoat—spinning flax—Bag [II, 106] of wool in one
corner—quantity of Linsey woolsey just
come home from weaver in the other—ears
of Indian corn & strings of dried apples hung
up—requested me[1] being a young man to call
the girl who was in the garden. Garden a
tangled enclosure with kitchen vegetables &
a few garish flowers. Girl a strong healthy
swarthy wench digging potatoes dressed in
but one garment scarcely necessary for de-
cency & applying her bare feet to the spade
—When she came in she was sent by the
mother to call her father who was ploughing
in the field. He came home in shirt—coarse
linen trousers seated sideways on a horse
taken from the plow. One [II, 105] leg
thrown over the Harness. paid him the
5000$ which he locked up in a large wooden
chest & returned to the plough. He was
building a large Brick house & thought of
having a Piazza round it.—Stated the reasons pro & con. & chiefly determined in favour of it because it would be such a favour-
able place to hang up the gears [?] in wet
weather

[1] Written above the phrase "requested me" are two
illegible words.

[II, 103] Virginia—

Difference between the men of the mountains & those of the plains. The former were hardy, open, vigorous & animated.

During the war when the peasantry was collected into encampments the difference was striking. The low landers lounged in groups —drawing figures in the sand—talking of fishing &c.—How they lived at home—of their rustic luxuries &c On going to the encampments of the mountain peasants found them pitching the bar—leaping &c Their conversation consisted of hunting stories adventures &c.—any thing hardy & animated— all their movements sprightly &c—

[II, 102] Preston lives in Washington county, on the Ledge of the Allegheny— where the western waters commence—Limestone Mountains coverd with trees except where a ridge of white rocks extend with trees hanging over them—

Broad rich valleys. Washington county abounding with minerals & every thing necessary to life

Tin Pedlars in Virginia—entertained at farmers houses all night & at morn rob the beds of three or 4 pounds of feathers—

Yankees took in the Virginians by selling

about 13,000 wooden clocks[1]—[II, 101] not
100 of which go at present.

One pedler [*sic*] stopped at farmers house
selling clocks—for note at 6 mo. and if clock
did not prove good when he came to collect the
note he would either take it back or change
it.

Clocks went for about 3 weeks & then got
out of order—various causes assigned—
When he came at end of 6 mo. he was pro-
vided with new clock. on the first person
complaining of his clock he exchg[d] it for the
new one & rec[d] pay[t] of note—He then went
thro his account taking clock of last person,
repairing it & exchang[g] it with the next &
thus at the expense of one new clock satisfied all his customers—always taking care to
stay a night to see that the new clock went
right

[II, 100] Virginia gent of the old times
generous, liberal, open, hospitable brave
courteous—every thing that could constitute
the gentleman—Their houses—Large Halls
where you find the tables that used to be coverd with plenty & hospitality open to the

---

[1] This is a characteristic instance of Irving's amusement at the shrewd Yankees. Compare the passages on
the Yankees in Diedrich Knickerbocker's *A History of
New York* (1809) and in *The Sketch Book* (1819-1820).

stranger broken & disjointed—Old Book
cases coverd with cobwebs odd vol of Spec-
tator—traces of former taste—the dregs of
a generous bottle—

The owners gone to Kentucky—

Old Mansions on James River—of wood—
some of Brick that was brought from England—

Soil worn out by tobacco vile weed—aban-
doned & returned to woods where the deer
resume their ancient haunts—

[I, 75] Effects of independent mode of
living in the Virginia climate, so independent, bountiful &c

[II, 89] Missouri & Mississippi[1]—former
turbid, yellowish & impetuous—latter pure
limpid & gentle—sometimes expanding into
lakes &c at their Junction   The Mississippi
seems to shrink from the abutment [?] of its
impetuous neighbour—is forced under the
opposite bank or rather seems to shrink under

---

[1] During his western tour Irving arrived in St. Louis
on September 12, 1832. A letter to Mrs. Paris, dated St.
Louis, September 13, 1832, describes his voyage down the
Ohio to the Mississippi: "I have been charmed with the
grand scenery of these two mighty rivers." *Life and Letters of Washington Irving*, III, 37. Possibly the two following notes were made during this period. Compare the
reference to the Missouri River in *Notes while preparing
Sketch Book &c.*, p. 62.

it and steal its coy & silver way along—unwilling to mingle its pure waters with the turbid waves of the Missouri—

Singular contrast of the impetuous flow of the rivers & the gentle descent of the countries—Some rivers run nearly from opposite. The Illinois for instance—each equally rapid —yet no apparent descent of the lands. Like torrents rushing from Diff^t Hills—Like Knights tilting at each other—

The Mississippi—when it gets among the low flats—after leaving the [II, 88] table (mountain) lands—& gets where it has made the alluvial soil—Seems higher than the soil —When on shore you see Vessels gliding above you.

[I, 90] Blustering young officer—swears and talks loudly[1]—

Arrival at the Camp—his idea of a military service to ride at full gallop in front of men, to harangue—to light [?] them up to deeds of valour &c &c—cold northern com-

---

[1] Although some of the following passages seem to suggest episodes in *Astoria* (1836) and *The Adventures of Captain Bonneville* . . ., I can find no proof that Irving so used them. Nor is their origin certain. In all probability they reflect experiences of Irving in the South in 1832 or 1833. The background for such experiences is made evident in the *Life and Letters of Washington Irving,* III, 33-44.

mander—common placed—orders given ve-
hemently [?]—no haranguing—no enemy to
see—but distant summons of Meeting [?]
hastens [?] every [?] horseman [?][1]—accompanied by a faithful negro—men discon-
tented about the quality of the provisions—

Joins troop of horse—Did not know how to
ride—had to have great exercise [I, 89] different characters of the troops those of the
lowlands & those of mountains

Young officers & volunteers continue to arrive—odd equipment—all want to get white
horses & to ride to the death [?] V cannot
get appoint[d] & acts as volunteer—a volunteer corps of cavalry—all for galloping drill
[?] for the picturesque—

His excursion to Kentucky—the Story of
Marse.[2]

The prospect from the top of the Allegheny—visit to the indian fortifications [I,
88] Modes of adventuring thro the wilderness and down the rivers

[I, 86] Mountaineers more attached to
their homes than those of the plains—because
there is more character about these bold

---

1 These phrases are blurred and almost illegible.
2 I have been unable to identify this story. Compare
Notes while preparing Sketch Book &c., p. 54.

prominences of Nature—strong scenery always attaches—there is a home a limit—Boundaries [?] that concentrate the view & keep the mind from wandering [?] about on a plain a man scarcely knows the limits of his home or what it is—It seems to extend to the end of the earth. he dissipates his mind & efforts in the boundless spaces of heaven & earth—Demands [?] of Nature are deepest. As I have observed in the human character, those who were of even temper & placid flat faces had many acquaintances & well wishers but an executive [?] man with strong features had warm friends. There is something wonderfully alluring in a roman nose

[I, 82] Every day new volunteers arrived They were young men of the best families high mettled, chivalrous—but nearly as ignorant of the woods as myself—tall gallant looking fellows Well mounted on blood horses —with negroes attending them. Their picturesque equipment—swords—pistols something or other of warlike import—

They were all for riding the white [?] horse & firing pistols into the air—I suspect their fathers had all battle pieces hanging in their halls.   Declamatory.

THE STORY OF ROSALIE

[I, 85] I have been settled 4 months and am perfectly satisfied with my situation The house is commodious & being a cabin will admit of wings being added as my family increases—I have set out shrubbery & trees which in a few years will give a fine big grove to my landscape[1]—

[1] This collection of puzzling notes is apparently the rough draft of a novel, and so has unusual significance in a study of Irving. It is evident from this notebook, and from hints elsewhere, that Irving, known as an essayist, experimented in the form of the novel as well as in that of the drama. These passages are almost illegible, and have cost many hours of study of handwriting. They are incoherent in their sequence; they are interrupted by other notations; and the whole scheme of Irving's projected story remains obscure. Yet the length of the tale, the variety of incident, and the caption "Last Chap" seem to indicate a narrative more ambitious even than "Dolph Heyliger," "Buckthorne and his Friends," or "Mountjoy." Some of the notes reappear in other essays. It is possible that Irving, abandoning his original plan for a novel, used thriftily his material, or parts of it, elsewhere. Yet no extensive adaptation of the story of Rosalie, or Rosy, appears in Irving's published works.

Sophy (Sophie) is the name of the devoted sister in "Mountjoy," in *The Crayon Miscellany*. "Mountjoy" bears indeed striking resemblances to these notes. The mentor, Glencoe, is in both, as are the smiling fathers; the philosophic heroes are very similar, and some details are strictly parallel: the gypsy hat, the study of Italian. Yet in the main there is great divergence.

The plot of the story of Rosalie, so far as it may be

[I, 84] I am now   [1] and am quietly
settled with my dear Rosie on the side of one
of the Alleghany, near the scene of our lives
& my day dreams. We have already a fine
little family around us—and I trust to pass
a happy life among them. As I was sitting in
front of the house the other evening watching
the setting sun, with Rosy seated beside me
on the bench, her arm resting on my shoulder
—watching the scene of evening splendour &
youthful mirth

I am now my dear Rosy said I at quiet with
all the world—I have happily got thro all
my follies & caprices and am safely anchored
—I have done work on the building. I will

reconstructed, is concerned with the love of a philosophical and mildly asinine young man for the volatile
Rosy. She is rescued, apparently from the Richmond
fire. The lover meets Rosy unexpectedly in society in
Philadelphia. There is a quarrel and a reconciliation.
We see the hero at home with his father and sisters.
Rosy goes to Kentucky. Another scene, presumably the
last, shows the lover and Rosy happy together in the
mountains, with their children about them. There are
other details, but their relation to the story is uncertain,
as is the order of the events here summarized. The passages have been reprinted in what appears to have been
Irving's original arrangement. In reproducing the story
only those details have been kept which are certainly
parts of the narrative of Rosalie. Others not demon-
strably links in it have been rigidly excluded. These are
given elsewhere with indications of their possible connection with the tale. See pp. 103, 108, footnote 2, 125.

[1] Irving's blank.

never change my mode of living but will devote myself to the rearing of those blessed little ones. I will form their minds from infancy that they shall not be so fickle as myself but determined particular persons [?] Charles who should [I, 83] study [?] solidly [?] shall be a lawyer—he cannot but rise at the bar & as to the rest of the children we shall have ———[1] well my dear Freder [ick?] said Rosy half weeping & half laughing I am glad to see you so reformed, but in the mean time had you not a will let the children build their air castles

Has had thoughts of aspiring for Congress Presidency—

[I, 80] Those who live in the world can have but faint idea of the love of that[2] of two beings thus secluded & surrounded by mountain wilderness—

they who live in cities and are surrounded by a whole firmament of beauty can have no idea of my loneliness when Rosy was away She was the silver moon of a starless[3] sky—they

[1] Apparently Irving's dash. Above "to" is written an illegible word.

[2] Three words, beginning with "love," have been crossed out.

[3] Eight words, beginning with "She," have been crossed out.

in the absence of the mistress of their affection—have all the lesser lights of heaven to
illumine them with the beams of beauty—but
Rosy was to me the moon of a starless sky—
when she withdrew her lovely countenance all
was darkness

[I, 78]¹ Rosy was to the full an —— but
women have a natural adroitness in society
—their minds as their bodies are more pliant
and facile of accomodation to her —— as I
launched out into the enthusiasm [?] of
party I saw her steal a shy but arch look
from among her locks at me and a smile steal
about her pretty little mouth it startled me—
I felt a momentary dread that she might²

[I, 77] Rosys father grown impoverished
& determines to go to Kentucky—

Fredericks visit to the deserted mansion—
to Rosys chamber.

His idea of settling in the wilderness with
Glencoe for a companion—

Battle scene where his men run & he is
wounded & taken prisoner—carried on board
a British ship of the line—

I have the odious habit of laughing in the

---

¹ Preceding this entry a page and two-thirds of a
page (I, 79, and I, 78) have been carefully rubbed out.
² The passage breaks off abruptly.

wrong place which had so often been my annoyance she cast her eyes down again however with a resumption of the most absolute demureness and I felt as ever ——[1]

nothing   of [?] that could surpass her countenance when her eyes were cast down under their long silken lashes—her ringlets hung in profusion [?] over her soft cheeks and she seemed listening with much attention to the words of wisdom I was uttering

[I, 76] Rosy had now & then a very equivocal way of darting sly and arch glances from under the covert of her clustering locks & gypsy bonnet. It was a kind of bush fighting that now & then took me most unexpectedly—[2]

[I, 75] Glencoe then serious [?] upon supernatural beings—who can tell what unseen beings walk their airy rounds among these mountains—The —— above are unknown—

The hooting of the owl

As he spoke of the deceased his voice often [?] in deep sepulchral tone.

[I, 73] Girls become wonderfully intimate

---

[1] In the next line three words are illegible.

[2] Compare these two entries with similar passages in "Mountjoy," *Wolfert's Roost,* pp. 83, 84.

on return home—Rosy & my sisters were
sworn friends—she loved my dear sister
Sophy to distraction—

[I, 72]—Last Chap—

Meets Rosy in Phila—on reconciliation &
conversation—I have now seen much of the
world & of mankind—years have brought
wisdom and experience.

I repeated to Rosy all that Glencoe had
said I tried to fly the metaphor [?] of the
eagle—but it would not pass—I felt like de-
votion—My father smiled

Talking with Glencoe about war. Interrupt
him with occasional thoughts about white
horses—volume of smoke.

—When he comes to picturesque part of
his discourse I listen more attentively ——[1]

[I, 71] Rosy in the evening she would
bend down to me & breathe one of her little
songs in my ear

Rosys figure—her figure [*sic*] certainly
was totally different from all I had imagined
but it answered a will [?] I thought her the
most beautiful being I had ever seen

[I, 64]　　Glencoe

I repaired to the house of her father & was

[1] The rest of the page is water-stained and has been
rubbed out.

admitted—they could not keep out wretched-
ness like mine—Beside there was no danger
of my machinations   she was yielding to the
grasp of a mere inevitable [?] specter—I
only came to see her perish.

I saw her die[1]—

I see her in lovely sunbeams—as often I
hear her tones in the echoes of these mountains—She is about my path.

A strange being visits me every night—he
enters in spite of my presence—he is bent
down & haggard & ——[2] he comes as the
darkness of the night & lays himself down
beside me—I cannot sleep—my [I, 63] rest
is gone I am beggard—broken down wretch

[I, 62] I [*sic*] sweet smile stole over her
face, it was a thoughtful & rather melancholy
one—she looked like pity smiling on a sinful
world.

[I, 61] My journey homeward recruited
my health—the specter that had haunted me
remained behind. The prospect of my return
to the alleghany cheered me up

---

1 This jotting, even in the midst of the sketch of
Rosy, recalls the other personal confessions in this notebook and in *Notes while preparing Sketch Book &c.* (see
pp. 63, 64). It is barely possible that Irving is thinking
of the death-scene of Matilda Hoffman, in 1809.

2 Two words are illegible.

—came covertly [into?] the Kitchen & sees
[?] them [?] all in full song—

My father received me kindly—there was a
lurking smile on his countenance which I
could not understand. My mother & sisters
wept over my pale & sunken cheeks and determined that I should go no more within
—— college that I should stay at home with
them for I know enough [?] My dear sister
Sophy wept over me a[nd?] I laid my tired
weary
[*sic*] head in her lap & was at peace

she was like a camelion—when she saw
me melancholy she would come by me &
breathe one of her little songs into my ear—

[I, 60] Sophy said I—I am in love[1]

I am surprised thot I to myself that Glencoe has never taught me italian—it is all important—what use is latin & such to me
nobody talks them—but here—as my very
pen intent [?] on the word italian is rhymed
in my face.   I will set about studying the
language on my return and —— I will study
German &c[2]

In her fair clear countenance a pure soul
shone as the perfect day

1 Compare "Mountjoy," p. 65.
2 Compare *ibid.,* pp. 96, 97. Three words in the last
sentence are illegible.

The light of love which —— burned in her sweet blue eyes

she played about me like summer lightning [I, 59] Latent accomplishment seemed to sleep in her & only to be awaked by accidental encounters. She was like the diamond continually flashing upon me some new light

She played around me—she delighted to sport my very [?] gravity—she would disappear with her whim & then come unexpectedly upon me with some [?] note of melting pathos

He had an uneasy [?] temper—he ——[1] and fancied that when he was fretting he was moralizing Philosophizing [I, 58] in philadelphia he enters into the dissipation of society — writes a poem on a lady which he inserts in a weekly paper read by all the milliners—he [?] is pronounced a sweet poet—and makes ——[2]

Hears of a great belle finds it is Rosalie unexpectedly she is surrounded by beaux— takes no notice of him. Sings a song about indifference

She dances cotillion—he looks on with burning eye—hates these unhallowed contacts—He never learned to dance—regrets it

[1] Five words are illegible.
[2] Two words are illegible.

—wishes he could descend from his dignity—
almost regrets that he is a philosopher.

His reconciliation with Rosy—mutual re-
proach she affects hatred—fickle—produces
the damning proof the Weekly Museum. her
pride gives way—she bursts into tears—

[I, 57] Her going brought to my mind
all our past scene of ——— all the innocent
endearments and early love among the wild
Valleys of the Alleghenys—

I became perfectly fascinated by her. She
shall turn the lighter grace of her mind
round my philosophical spirit—I will be the
stately pillar of the home & she the light
wreath that graces it.

[I, 54] you have seen [?] of Rosalie—you
have a world [?] a worthless, heartless and in
exchange go reap your harvest of shallow
smiles your [*sic*] and say if one true heart
rooted affection is not worth them all

Rescues Rosalie from fire at Rich^d   sees
her from opposite box—shrieks & ———¹ escapes out of the window   she faints   alarm
of Mr Somerville—flame expires in the silver
light of a moonbeam

His disconsolate return to college

¹ Five words are illegible.

PERSONALIA:

READING, WRITING, AND MISCELLANEOUS NOTES

[I, 47] Jan 1, 1818. At Springfield. Birmingham—remarkable frosty morning—there had been fog which was precipitated by the cold and coverd all the trees & every blade of grass with frost. like fine snow[1]—

[I, 71] recollect my leaping in the streets of Baltimore by Moonlight—clapping my hands & exclaiming let me but be renowned[2]

[I, 83] Fond of Angling—suited my musing habits—

[I, 87] My father dubbed me the Philosopher from my lonely & abstracted habits—but I was the least of a philosopher as a boy[3]

[1] Irving was in Liverpool on December 23, 1817, and again, apparently, on January 27, 1818. This note was, perhaps, written on a visit to the home of his sister, Mrs. Henry Van Wart, at Birmingham. See *Life and Letters of Washington Irving*, I, 392, 394. It is, in these notebooks, the only specific reference to the year 1818.

[2] Perhaps autobiographical or part of the story of Rosalie, in the midst of which it occurs. The same comment may be made concerning the next three entries. See also "The Angler," *The Sketch Book*, pp. 440-452.

[3] The first of these two sentences is probably autobiographical, the second certainly so. "At the age of

Robinson Cruesoe [*sic*]—Sinbad the Sailor
—led to read voyages & travels—that of running away & going to sea—fixed myself in a
regiment [?] but hated pork [?] & gave it
up

[I, 88] My anticipations of success at the
Bar how I would overwhelm the guilty—up-
hold the innocent—I would scarcely have
changed my anticipation for the fame of
Cicero   he was too cold &c[1]

[I, 96] I have repeatedly applied for some
paltry public situation but have been as often
disappointed—It has pleased heaven that I
should be driven on upon my inner strength
—and resort to the citadel [?] within me[2]

[I, 70] why should I go home—what home

eleven," says Pierre Irving, "books of voyages and
travels became his passion. This feeling was first awakened by the perusal of Robinson Crusoe and Sinbad the
Sailor." *Life and Letters of Washington Irving*, I, 32.

[1] This entry is especially interesting in view of Irving's failure as a lawyer. He entered the law office of
Henry Masterton of New York in 1799. In 1801 he was
employed by Brockholst Livingston, and in 1802 he became clerk under Josiah Ogden Hoffman. On November
21, 1806, he was admitted to the bar. He then gradually
drifted away from active practice into literature. See
ibid., I, 37-173.

[2] This note reflects a recurrent mood of Irving prior
to the success of *The Sketch Book*. His brothers were
endeavoring to secure employment for him. See his
letter to William Irving, Liverpool, December 23, 1817,
and that to Ebenezer Irving (Undated. November ?
1818). *Ibid.*, I, 393, 409.

have I—I carry my home with me, it is the world of my thoughts, it is peopled with the memories of those I loved—it is filled with faces of women & looks of friendship—with friends that have sunk into the grave & darkness [?] that have passed to heaven

Why return to see the changes from places in desolation—to see   ¹ to knock at the doors of the —— [I, 69] and be [?] received by strange faces. to find   ² to enquire for the abode of youth & gaity & content [?] and to be led to the tombstone

buried love

[I, 83] The oppressive heat of a summers day—& yet it was to me delicious to lie under a broad tree on a rich clover bank and look up into the deep blue vault—to have a book & read while the cricket would skip into my book the busy ant hurry across my page & the bee buzz with venom [?] —what delicious slumber have I had with a book on my head.

[II, 1] Dʳ Barrows works edited by Tillotson³

¹ Irving's blank.
² Irving's blank.
³ Irving probably used *The Works of Isaac Barrow,* published by the Rev. Dr. Tillotson, London, 1683-1687.
After this entry are two others consisting of sixteen words, of which only the following are legible: "Brevoort Nicholson Wᵐ Hoffman Kemble Newman Parry Strand."

[II, 7] Sir Wm Temple[4]

Many friends may do one little good one enemy much hurt.

Leisure & solitude, the best effect of Riches because mother of thought. Both avoided by most rich men, who seek company & business, which are signs of being weary of themselves.

The only way for a rich man to be healthy is by exercise & abstinence to live as if he were poor, which are esteemed the worst parts of poverty

The first ingredient in conversation is Truth, the next good sense, the third good humour, & the fourth wit.

When I consider how many noble and estimable men, how many lovely and agreeable women I have outlived among my acquaintance & friends methinks it looks impertinent to be still alive.

[II, 8] Changes in veins of wit like those of habits or other modes.

[II, 9]   These were his traits of worth
                 And must we lose them now
            And shall the scene no more show forth
                 His sternly pleasing brow—

            Alas the moral brings a tear—
                 Tis all a transient hour below
            And we that would detain thee here
                 Ourselves as fleetly go—

---

[4] These six quotations, with minor alterations in punctuation, capitalization, and spelling, may be found in *The Works of Sir William Temple*, London, 1814. See III, 533, 532, ". . . the Different Conditions of Life and Fortune"; and 543, 545, "Heads Designed for an Essay on Conversation."

Fair as some classic dome
Robust and richly graced
Your Kembles spirit was the home
Of genius and of taste

Taste like the silent dials power
That when supernal light is given
Can measure inspirations hour
And tell its height in heaven

[II, 10] His was the spell oer hearts
Which only acting lends
The youngest of the sister arts
Where all their beauty blends

For ill can poetry express
Full many a tone or thought sublime
And painting mute & motionless
Steals but one glance from time

But by the mighty Actor brought
Illusions wedded triumphs come
Verse ceases to be airy thought
And sculpture to be dumb—

But who forgets that white discrowned
head
Those bursts of reasons half extin-
guished glare
Those tears upon Cordelias bosom shed
In doubt more touching than despair[1]

1 All these lines are from "Valedictory Stanzas to
J. P. Kemble, Esq. Composed for a Public Meeting,
Held June, 1817," in *The Poetical Works of Thomas
Campbell, with Notes, and a Biographical Sketch,* by the
Rev. W. A. Hill, London, 1851, pp. 138-140. The stanzas

[II, 114] Funeral processions—service &c
vide Hooker on Ecclesiastical polity Book V
—paragraph 75 &c

Women apt to follow new doctrines—Preface to Hookers Work above-mentioned[1]

Hoopers Sermon—on the text If they hear
not Moses & the prophets &c[2]

[II, 112] Various circumstances had occasioned to give a melancholy tone to the public mind & to excite the public imagination—
The Dreadful conflagration of the Theatre
of Richmond[3] which had wrapped beauty &

are in different order from that of the original, and
there are minor alterations in spelling, punctuation,
and capitalization. Irving was much interested in the acting of Kemble. Allusions to him occur frequently in
Irving's correspondence. See also small notebook, blue
paper duodecimo, dated 1806, in the Seligman Collection,
New York Public Library.

I am indebted to Mr. Horace Howard Furness, Jr., of
Philadelphia, for assistance in identifying this poetry by
Campbell.

[1] These two notes may be traced with some certainty
to Hooker's prose. See *The Works of Mr. Richard
Hooker, Containing Eight Books of Laws of Ecclesiastical Polity* . . ., Oxford, 1843, I, 125-127; and II, 70-74.

[2] Probably George Hooper (1640-1727), Bishop of
Bath and Wells. I have been unable to locate this sermon.

[3] Since the burning of the Richmond Theatre took
place on December 26, 1811, the setting of this episode
is late in this year or early in 1812. The story was not,
then, obviously, gleaned by Irving on his visit to Richmond in 1807. He was again in Virginia in 1833, and
may have heard the story at that time. More probably
it is an anecdote derived from a friend or a book. A

talents in flames. Tornado which had swept the southern coast & desolated the country &c The continual succession of earthquakes—all had produced a feverish excitement & filled the imagination with dreams of horror & apprehensions of sinister & dreadful events

About this time a man published a prophesy—predicting the end of the world on 4 June. effect of it on the country people Work suspended many did not grow corn for they knew not that they should reap it—In the town where our [II, 111] college was situated a Butcher had been made the depository of many of the pamphlets—He was resorted to by all those of diseased & alarmed minds—from continually reading them & conversing with every variety of melancholy & forlorn being his intellects became confused & he went mad.

The diseased state of the public mind was caught in the college. some went home others lodged about in small wooden houses.—Some took up a desperate mode of dissipating thought & played cards incessantly—One

search of books available to Irving has not revealed this passage. Irving did not apparently use the episode in his published writings. The passage may even be a part of the story of Rosalie. Compare the reference to the Richmond fire on p. 102.

man was stationed at a pendulum to give warning of the approach of [II, 110] a shock —that we might fly to the fields. He got a bugle & used to sound three blasts. Never did any thing sound to me more disastrous—He was nicknamed *Gabriel* by one of the profligates. I used to take my bible & read.

Alarm of earthquake at night. We all fled to the college court. Chimney falls with dreadful crash—exclamation that the earth had opened before us—lurid look of the heaven—stillness & oppressiveness of air Wall of one of the bigger apartments falls —Exclamation that the earth had opened. behind—dreadful state of [II, 109] alarm. Meteor streams over the College. Glare a baleful light over the court yard & bursts with tremendous report—gave myself up for lost— thought I was annihilated—

Howling of dogs Screams of domestic fowls—Shrieks of women & wailing of children

Butcher runs frantically about the street foaming at the mouth—& crying Woe Woe Woe the destruction of Columbia is at hand &c—prepare for the presence of the Lord

Shrieks of women—all was awe & dismay—

[I, 32] There is an endeavour among some of the writers of the day (who fortunately have not any great weight.) to introduce into poetry all the common colloquial phrases and vulgar idioms—In their rage for simplicity they would be coarse and commonplace. Now the Language of poetry cannot be too pure and choice. Poems are like classical edifices, for which we seek the noblest materials—what should we think of the work of the architect who would build a Grecian temple of brick when he could get marble[1]—

Leigh Hunts Rimini[2] shows a heterogeneous taste—in which a fondness for gorgeous material is mingled up with an occasional proneness [?] to the most grotesque—we fancy him a common stone mason with dirty apron & trowel in hand sometimes building with marble & sometimes with rubbish—

[1] Perhaps an allusion to Wordsworth and his followers. Although Irving lived on until 1859, a witness of the significant changes in conceptions of English poetry, to these he remained indifferent. He consistently preferred Moore, Scott, or Byron to Wordsworth, Shelley, or Keats. Irving as a critic of literature was conventional, and without unusual powers of analysis. The idiom of the "stone mason" he repeats in *Notes while preparing Sketch Book &c.,* p. 57.

[2] *The Story of Rimini* appeared in 1816. Compare Irving's reference to Leigh Hunt in *Notes while preparing Sketch Book &c.,* p. 57.

[I, 33] His[1] writings are like those edifices which one occasionally sees in italy— where the architect has purloined the fragments of ancient tables and mingled them with his own rubbish in building his walls.

[II, 85] Byrons poems fragment of a genius

giant mind   like fragments of a column give an idea of the grandeur of the whole[2]—

parting [?] Spring—

[II, 5] The closest union here cannot last longer than death us depart; wherefore no man upon such account can truly call or heartily esteem himself happy. Why then do we so cumber our heads with care, so rack our hearts with passion, so waste our spirits with incessant toil about these transitory things? Why do we so highly value, so ardently desire, so eagerly pursue so fondly delight in, so impatiently want or love, so passionately contend for & emulate one another in regard to these bubbles, forfeiting

[1] Irving is still speaking of Leigh Hunt.

[2] Irving's interest in Byron was unflagging. Compare the mentions of him in *Notes while preparing Sketch Book &c.*, p. 82, and in the printed correspondence in the *Life and Letters of Washington Irving, passim.* The most complete expression of this interest is in "Newstead Abbey," *The Crayon Miscellany*, pp. 323-441.

& foregoing our home bred most precious
good, tranquility & repose—either of mind
or body for them? Why erect such mighty
fabricks of expectation & confidence upon
such unsteady sands Why dress we up these
our Inns as if they were our homes & are as
careful about a few nights lodgings here as if
we designed an everlasting abode. For we are
but sojourners & pilgrims here, and [we?]
have no fixed habitation upon earth who, who
come forth like ——

[I, 29] Man must be aspiring: ambition
belongs to his nature. He cannot rest content
but is continually to [*sic*] reaching after
higher attainments and more felicitous conditions. To rest satisfied with the present is a
sign of an abject spirit—it is the attribute
of the soul to continually spring upwards and
seek after perfections unattainable in this
short life—it is a proof of its immortality—
Every being has the propensity towards that
state for which it is created—some animals
never raise their eyes above the earth on which
they are destined to grovel—while the young
eaglet[1] darts upward his keen gaze. balances
his wings & shews all the aspiring propen-

[1] Irving is fond of this image. Compare *Notes while
preparing Sketch Book &c.,* p. 67.

sities of a bird that is one day to soar into the Skies.

[I, 31] N——[1] was a man of Society— buoyant, and communicative. He visit^d universally—and was continually abroad. He dissipated himself upon society and had no time for reflection. He impaired his dignity of character—for such is the ungratefulness of society that it always esteems those least who are most devoted to it.

A more reserved character, one who lives more with & more for himself is much more dignified & much more respected, yet I scarcely know whether he is so useful He is like a stream that runs in one deep channel, possessing dignity of flow & singleness of character—The other like a stream diverted into a garden & distributed into rills that visit every flower—the former is most beautiful in itself—the latter is diffusive in its benefits & spreads freshness and cheerfulness around.

[I, 50] Emmet. 1803

[1] The dash is Irving's. It is barely possible that this note alludes to Stuart Newton, whom Irving met in 1818. See *Life and Letters of Washington Irving,* I, 406. The passage suggests similar ones in the *Notes while preparing Sketch Book &c.,* pp. 86, 87, and in the essay "Roscoe." See *The Sketch Book,* p. 32.

Arrested in Aug wounded as he attempted to escape   tried Sept 14 & 19.

If the spirits of the illustrious dead participate in the concerns & care of those who were dear to them in this transitory life—Oh! ever dear and venerated shade of my departed father, look down with scrutiny upon the conduct of your suffering son, & see if I have even for a moment deviated from those principles of morality & patriotism which it was your care to instill into my youthful mind and for which I am now to offer up my life.

My lord you seem impatient for the sacrifice the blood for which you thirst is not congealed by the artificial terrors which surround your victim; it circulates warmly & unruffled through the channels which God created for noble purposes but which you are bent to destroy for purposes so grievous that they cry to heaven—Be yet patient! I have but a few words more to say—I am going to my cold and silent grave: my lamp of life is nearly extinguished: my race is run: the grave opens to receive me and I sink into its bosom—I have but one request to ask at my departure from this world; it is the charity of its silence—Let no man write my epitaph, for as [I, 49] no man who knows my motives dare *now* vindicate them let not prejudice or ignorance asperse them—Let them and me repose in obscurity, and my tomb remain uninscribed, until other times & *other men* can do justice to my character—When my country takes her place among the nations of the earth *then* and not till then let my epitaph be written—I HAVE DONE!¹

[I, 36] Daughter of Curran engaged to Emmet who was hanged for treason. Her father fearing his loyalty should be suspected literally turned her out of doors. She was received into the home of friends. Her brokenheartedness—pined away. At masquerade where others were gay she would sit down on the steps of orchestra and sing a little simple melancholy air with such pathos as to draw a crowd round her & melt every one into tears. She was addressed by an officer in the army but declined his addresses her heart was buried in Emmets grave. He persisted & married her. Went to Sicily—She however pined

¹ No text of Emmet's speech has been found which duplicates in every particular Irving's version in this notebook. Two texts, however, are identical with it, except for two or three words, and a few marks of punctuation. It is more than possible that Irving consulted one of these, and erred in transcribing these two or three phrases. They are "Insurrection of 1803, Conducted by Robert Emmett [*sic*], Esq.," in *The History of the Late Grand Insurrection; Or, Struggle for Liberty in Ireland* . . ., Carlisle, 1805, pp. 351, 352; and a pamphlet, *The Speech of Robert Emmet, Esq. As Delivered at the Sessions House, Dublin,* . . . London, n.d. [1814?], p. 8. There exist numerous other versions of the speech. See, for example, D. J. O'Donoghue, *Life of Robert Emmet,* Dublin, 1902, pp. 174, 175.

away & died—of a broken heart—Moors [*sic*]
verses to her memory.[1]

—Instances of women dieing of love I believe are frequent They pine in thought &
waste away their death is attribut[d] to other
causes, but it is the shy ——[2] that preys
on their spirits makes them neglect all the
cheerful exercises that gladden the spirits &
diffuse healthful animation

[I, 37] Men dissipate their griefs in the
bustle & business of the world. Women are
more lonely—secluded—their life is more a
life of sentiment & affections. Early deaths
of consumption may often be traced to the
effects of disappointed love, preying on the
heart destroying the rest necessary for the
body and drying up the blood—

[1] This paragraph is a fairly complete outline of "The
Broken Heart," in *The Sketch Book,* pp. 98-105. The
succeeding paragraph, representing Irving's reflections
on the story, he employed as an introduction to the
actual incident, which begins: "Every one must recollect
the tragical story of young E——, the Irish patriot;
. . ." The essay ends with the verses of Moore:

> She is far from the land where her young hero sleeps,
> And lovers around her are sighing:
> But coldly she turns from their gaze, and weeps,
> For her heart in his grave is lying. . . .

Irving has retained some of the phraseology of the notebook, as in the image of the wounded dove. See *The
Sketch Book,* p. 100.

[2] Two words are illegible.

Man rushes [?] into society—woman like stricken dove wounded $\overset{bird}{\underset{dove}{}}$ [*sic*] carries her miseries into solitude, broods over the inward pang and pines away in silence[1]

[I, 39] There is something in sickness that softens the heart & brings it back to the tender feelings of childhood. Who that has suffered in advanced life in sickness or some loneliness [?] but has thought of the mother that looked on his childhood that smoothed his pillow of sickness & administered to his helplessness

The purest & strongest affection that winds itself round the human heart is that between the mother & the son—she will sacrifice all her comforts for him—she will love & cherish him in adversity—in disgrace—when all the world beside casts him off she will be all the world to him—She loses all the selfishness of human nature

[I, 40] As George told his story the old woman would look wistfully in his face—adjust his neckcloth—He will yet be cured [?] she looked fondly at him as if she would fain read confirmation in his countenance but

[1] This paragraph, part of the same entry, receives its final form in "The Broken Heart," *The Sketch Book,* pp. 98-101.

death had written his doom to [*sic*] strongly there even for a mothers hopes—a hectic colour on his cheek.

His manly frankness as he talked with his mother as he died

When I saw her feebly quitting the church yard & leaving behind her the mouldy reliques of all that was dear on earth—returning to silence & destitution—my heart yearned over her—What are the distresses of the rich—they have friends to sooth [*sic*] pleasures to beguile—a crowd to divert & distract them smiles to rob sorrow of its sting & heaven of its —— but the sorrows of the [I, 41] poor—who have lost all that could sweeten the cup of life—the sorrows of a solitary aged destitute widow over an only son.

I must pursue the story to the last scene ——[1] return home melts me

What are the distresses of the young—the lively spirit pours its balms into the wound[2]

[I, 53] Glenth—[?] I have walked among the solitude of these mountains and fancied I heard the voices of departed friends calling

[1] Three words are illegible.

[2] These memoranda were made for "The Widow and Her Son," *The Sketch Book,* pp. 143-152. The finished passages follow (not in the order of the essay). A com-

to me in the ether—the grave has closed
on my early hopes,—My companions &
friends have gone into the land of forgetful-
ness—I am a lonely melancholy man—a
stranger & a sojourner in a foreign land—
no one cares for me on earth but I trust that
there are gentle spirits that look down on me
from heaven—that watch over my slumbers
and shed comfort on my path—

parison suggests Irving's habit of polishing the notes,
by the use of more "literary" words.

There is something in sickness that breaks down the pride of man-
hood; that softens the heart, and brings it back to the feelings of infancy. Who that has languished, even in advanced life, in sickness
and despondency; who that has pined on a weary bed in the neglect
and loneliness of a foreign land; but has thought on the mother "that
looked on his childhood," that smoothed his pillow, and administered to his helplessness? Oh! there is an enduring tenderness in the
love of a mother to her son that transcends all other affections of the
heart. It is neither to be chilled by selfishness, nor daunted by danger, nor weakened by worthlessness, nor stifled by ingratitude. She
will sacrifice every comfort to his convenience; she will surrender
every pleasure to his enjoyment; she will glory in his fame, and ex-
ult in his prosperity; —and, if misfortune overtake him, he will be
the dearer to her from misfortune; and if disgrace settle upon his
name, she will still love and cherish him in spite of his disgrace; and
if all the world beside cast him off, she will be all the world to him.

The passage in the notebook beginning: "As George
told his story," Irving did not use in the essay. His
final version of the next passage follows:

When I saw the mother slowly and painfully quitting the grave,
leaving behind her the remains of all that was dear to her on earth,
and returning to silence and destitution, my heart ached for her.

The last passage he definitely altered:

But the sorrows of the poor, who have no outward appliances to
soothe,—the sorrows of the aged, with whom life at best is but a
wintry day, and who can look for no after-growth of joy,—the sorrows of a widow, aged, solitary, destitute, mourning over an only
son, the last solace of her years: these are indeed sorrows which
make us feel the impotency of consolation.

The silver pomp of heaven at night[1]

[II, 114] Robustness of eng character—
habits persons & minds less sensibility to what
is graceful & beautiful. Fond of order—neat-
ness cleanliness [?]—absence of enthusiasm
—not very excitable—no poetical character[2]

[I, 35] Noble avenues of trees to old
family mansions—Like sylvan collonades
[*sic*]—grand & imposing effect—

Old style of gardening—flights of steps
artificial terraces—statues—urns—cumbrous
ballustrades of stone with occasionally a pea-
cock with its long fluttering train—

[I, 46] Apollo of Belvidere french copies
of it taken —— all approximating nearly to
each other until they came down to a Bull-

---

[1] It is probable that from these notes Irving derived much of "St. Mark's Eve," in *Bracebridge Hall*.
Personal as that essay is, this note is more so. There is
little repetition of phrase, save, perhaps: "What could
be more consoling than the idea that the souls of those
whom we once loved were permitted to return and watch
over our welfare? That affectionate and guardian spirits
sat by our pillows when we slept, keeping a vigil over
our most helpless hours?" There is, however, a striking
similarity in the words of the next entry. These in the
essay read: ". . . and the moon rising in her silent maj-
esty, and leading up all the silver pomp of heaven." See
Bracebridge Hall, pp. 149-151.

[2] This note suggests many passages in Irving's writings. See "Rural Life in England," *The Sketch Book*,
p. 91. Two succeeding items, of two words each, are
illegible.

frog—so reports passing from mouth to mouth—

[I, 48] The purest waters of contentment flow from those well [?] springs that are found in the secluded spots of domestic life— but he who seeks to drink out of the capricious stream of public favour will too often find the channel dry & dusty—

[I, 88] Pond, a wooden Bridge over an outlet of the pond where we sometimes leand to see the green frog dart thro the water and the tribes [?] of newts & terrapins—[1]

[I, 96] I haunted the spot—it was uncommonly beautiful—The brook made a broad bend and ran dancing & sparkling among pebbles—There was a wall of grey rock that sprang up through the opposite [?] trees I found it had a Seat [?]—this was a discovery I brought my book [?] here & delighted to —— [2] I meditated continually on the little footprints—what was the being that had thus passed by as in a cloud & merely left the print of a foot for me to worship—No —— that finds the fairy ring in the morning[3]

1 Compare "Mountjoy," *Wolfert's Roost,* p. 53.

2 Five words are illegible.

3 Compare *ibid.,* pp. 53, 63. This passage has been crossed out, but is here reproduced as a possible source of the essay, "Mountjoy."

[I, 43] Old Mr Ross of Ross river [?] father of Gen¹ Ross who was killed at Baltimore: was the great man of a small neighborhood in Ireland—There was a protestant church there, but the congregation was small, as the lower classes in the vicinity were principally catholic—the parson had a high opinion of Mr Ross, who was the patron of the church—The latter would sometimes fall asleep during the sermon—The clergyman out of respect to his patron would pause in his sermon. The old gent would wake & exclaim with a gentle wave of the hand—Go on Sir go on—I'm with you—

[I, 44] A small catholic chapel in Ireland being newly built the Bishop came down to consecrate it—In the meantime however service had been performed in it—The Bishop asked how they came to perform service in it before it was consecrated—Oh please your honour it has been consecrated—consecrated & who consecrated it. Macomb [?] please your worship—Macomb [?]—& who the devil consecrated Macomb [?]—

[I, 48] Old Dutch farmer near Jamaica (L I). benevolent—Justice of the peace—only had one culprit before him—his trouble of mind—culprit escapes, great Joy of the

justice (——— peace & the culprit) everything
raised & manufactured on the farm for house
supplies—

Go to his daughters to Tea—Hot cakes.
Sweetmeats, honey—pie &c &c.

VanNess & the Seat at Kinderhook—old
farm house—Big tree & spring—Jesse Mar-
vin [*sic*] Old Hoos The congressman &c—[1]

[I, 51] Most men can become familiar with
the rustic [?] bases of the columns while their
vision cannot reach to the beauties of its co-
rinthian capital

[I, 35] Asthmatical fellows request that
there should be no stone built over his grave
but a railing to keep people from trampling
on him

[I, 38] that break down the pride of mankind & the hard wind of—

[I, 38] He'll one day get the post obit

---

[1] This is the record of an episode which occurred apparently as early as 1808 or 1809. Irving describes it
fully in a letter to Jesse Merwin, dated Sunnyside, Feb-
ruary 12, 1851. (The original letter is now in the posses-
sion of Mr. Seymour Van Santvoord, of Troy, New
York.) If this entry was made at the time of the incident, this notebook of 1817 may include entries of a
much earlier period. Jesse Merwin was the prototype
of Ichabod Crane; the "congressman" was Congressman
Van Alen; and Hoos was a familiar name in the vicinity
of Kinderhook.

reward of an author. Hell die by & bye &
then theyl give him a funeral & build him a
monument[1]

[I, 90] Acc^t [Account?] of the education
& attainments of his sisters—[2]

[II, 81] Mr Trotter[3]—Was at the same
school with Scott—Scott was not remarkable
at school—Was very good humoured and
blythe at play. Old Fraser at Edinburgh was
the schoolmaster.

Scotts uncle [?] says he did not show any
poetic talent until 25 years of age

[II, 80] ride from Johnstown to Dutch
Settlement see Dutch Inn &. Yankee Settlement[4]

[I, 22] a genius that sprang from one of
the open [?] embraces of nature by the way-
side

[I, 23] Prestons story of his uncle telling
a learned lady of a gent riding hard—falling
& thinking his leg shot off—tied it up rode
home & next day it was as well as ever—never
had any pain in it since—lady endeavors to

[1] Compare "Buckthorne and His Friends," in *Tales
of a Traveller,* for other opinions of Irving on literary
reputation.

[2] This may be a part of the story of Rosalie.

[3] Compare p. 22.

[4] Irving visited Johnstown in 1800, 1802, and 1803. See
Life and Letters of Washington Irving, I, 39, 45, 48.

account [?] for it after some time by Sending
new one. I should have mentioned it was a
wooden leg. A wooden head &.

Young N. in love with little print of a
ladies foot[1]

[I, 82] The —— of the eagle struck me I
was impressed with the weight of what he
said—This may not be pleasing counsel said
I, but it is at least sound philosophy.[2]

[I, 111] Tannahill of paisley—Weaver[3]

[I, 70] Was covered with grape vines—
Broad leaves & Beechwood bark for cover-
ing tents

Elk—

Sweetbriar—Honeysuckle[4]

Light spiral foliage of the vine

crimson buds—

Silvery gleam of the dewy landscape by
Moonlight—thin haze of the valley—

[I, 44] Family of little ones. father acting [?] like the parent bird that runs at [?]
will [?] in quest of food

[1] Perhaps the idea which is found in "Mountjoy,"
Wolfert's Roost. Compare p. 122.

[2] Compare p. 113. In this passage Irving first wrote
the word "story." Later he deleted this word and sub-
stituted one which is illegible.

[3] Compare pp. 66, 67.

[4] Compare these phrases with those in "Mountjoy," p.
52.

[I, 65] he that can pour the light of song
& the charms of freedom [?] around his native land—

[I, 45] When dust has returned to dust &
the very monument becomes a ruin

for the memory of man passes away he
returns to dust & his very monument becomes
a ruin

[I, 52] under a despotic govt man only
lives for himself for he is a slave but under
a free govt he who lives only for himself is a
brute.

[II, 113] Preaching & praying of the
Methodists—lights of churches not extinguished for months

[II, 88] Prestons comparison of the whirl
of indistinct ideas of men in a city—

Opticians say that distribute colours sepa-
rately on a wheel & whirl it round—it produces no colour—so the constant whirl of sen-
sation produces no thought—

Since we cannot dart one certain glance
into the future or drag back one moment of
the past

[II, 87] Vron [?] at the Bren [?]
Ed—Jones—[1]

[1] In his seventy-sixth year Irving wrote William C.
Preston: "Your allusions to Jones of the Brinn and

Valle   crucis   evening
light clouds scudding over the valley across
the clear sky—cottage smoke curling—rush
of small stream

Greystone of the mountains

Mountains naked—grey with dusty green[1]

[I, 77] borne along on the —— notes
of the wipporwill [*sic*]—the scream of wild
geese as they flew over head lost in the dark
depths of heaven—[2]

[II, 3]   A snake baked a Hoe cake
            & set the frog to mind it.
            The Frog fell asleep
            & The lizard came & stole it.

            Bring back my hoe cake
            You long tail[d] nanny.[3]

Loch Katrine, brought up a host of recollections of
pleasant scenes and of pleasant adventures which we
enjoyed together in our peregrinations in England and
Scotland, in our younger days." *Life and Letters of
Washington Irving,* IV, 288.

1 The word after "Valle" is nearly illegible. If, as is
probable, Irving writes of Valle Crucis Abbey, near
Llangollen, the note may be a record of a walking tour
made in Wales with Preston in June, 1815 (see *ibid.,* I,
368). We know of Irving's visit there on Thursday, August 10, in that year. *The Journals of Washington Irving*
(from July, 1815, to July, 1842), edited by William P.
Trent and G. S. Hellman, Boston, 1919, I, 11.

2 Compare "Mountjoy," *Wolfert's Roost,* p. 53.

3 A southern negro song with an interesting history.
To numerous experts on American negro folk lore it is
apparently unknown. Two correspondents have informed

Old Faddy

[II, 74] Lets talk of graves, of worms, & epitaphs"

Richd II[1]

Roslin castle   12.6

Bill at MacGregors   11.10.2

[II, 77] Walsh's Review[2]

—William Robinson & Sons—

Liverpool—

Constable gives Jeffrey Tooth picks.

Scotts different employments as clerk-sheriff &c about 1700£ yet 12,000 will be up

me that they were taught it in childhood in the South. One of these quotes four variants on the stanzas. Professor Newman I. White, of Duke University, refers in a letter to a version of the jingle in T. W. Tally, *Negro Folk Rhymes,* New York, 1922, p. 49. This verse was probably learned by Irving during his southern journey. See also *The Negro Singers' Own Book,* Philadelphia [1846?], p. 329.

My thanks are due, in the study of this verse, to Professor White, and to Professor Addison Hibbard, of the University of North Carolina.

[1] A quotation from Shakespeare, *King Richard the Second,* III, ii, 145.

[2] Robert Walsh was at one time or another the editor of at least three magazines or reviews: *The American Register, or Summary review* . . ,; *The American Register, or General repository* . . .; and *The American Quarterly Review.* For allusions to Walsh see the correspondence of Henry Brevoort and Irving. See especially: *Letters of Henry Brevoort to Washington Irving,* edited by G. S. Hellman, New York, 1918, pp. 4, 5; and the *Letters of Washington Irving to Henry Brevoort,* edited by G. S. Hellman, New York, 1918, p. 35.

[II, 83] Ive had a gay bit nap.

Theres something no canny about the box.[1]

—— take a warlock &—[2]

Mr. Isaac Allison of Northumberland Large man who had been a fisherman & owned shipping[3]

Pass Dunstanborough Castle[4]

[II, 82] Hume Castle—Willy Wassel

> Willy Wassel
> Stands in his castle
> & defies the King & all his men
> to come & take it from him again[5]

Roxborough Castle—

Dunstanborough Castle

[I, 30] Wallaces cave[6]—Craig

[II, 65] strand

[I, 54] $\frac{\text{family vault}}{\text{family } [sic]}$ in M[r] Jones Garden

[II, 20] monument ——[7]

[II, 53] Old black woman at M[r] Kembles pointing at the clock—

[1] Compare p. 25.
[2] Two words are illegible.
[3] Compare p. 22.
[4] Compare p. 25.
[5] Perhaps an allusion to Burns'

> Willie Wastle dwalt on Tweed,
> The spot they ca'd it Linkumdoddie. . . .

[6] Compare pp. 49, 71.
[7] The rest of the line is illegible.

[II, 2] Books for HM[1]

Wilkinsons Memoirs	10.60—
Cleavelands Mineralogy	3.—
Pitkins Statistics	3.—
Drakes Cincinnati—	—80
American Register	1.—
Darbys Louisiana & Map	6.—
Walshs Register	2.50
Brackenridge Louisiana	2.—
———	60
	$29.50

Walshs [?] Map ——— = $10

[1] I have been unable to identify the person for whom this list was made. The books were, presumably: James Wilkinson, *Memoirs of My Own Times,* Philadelphia, 1816; Parker Cleaveland, *Elementary Treatise on Mineralogy and Geology,* . . . Boston, 1816; Timothy Pitkin, *A Statistical View of the Commerce of the United States,* . . . Hartford, 1816; Daniel Drake, *Notices Concerning Cincinnati,* . . . Cincinnati, 1810; *The American Register; or Summary Review of History, Politics, and Literature,* Philadelphia, 1817; William Darby, *A Geographical Description of the State of Louisiana,* . . . Philadelphia, 1816; *The American Register, or General Repository of History, Politics and Science,* Philadelphia and Baltimore, 1806-1810; H. M. Brackenridge, *Views of Louisiana,* . . . Pittsburgh, 1814.

*tle Dowie Dens of Yarrow where Scott was murd^d by
Kinsmen*

Beneath is this note, not in the handwriting of Irving:
*Memoranda made by Washington Irving of Sunnyside in
Scotland 1817.* Other writing is obliterated. Continuing
on page 128, there are two small sketches of flowers.
Then occur these notes: *Loch Lomond Inch Caliach
[Cailliach] burying place of the McGregors near Kill-
earn cottage where Buchanan was born Glen Fruin
scene of the conflict in which the McGregors were de-
stroyed—here* [three words illegible] *also home* [?] *of
Smollett craig Roslin* [?]—*rendezvous of Rob Roy
enemy of Duke of Montrose—north of Inversnaid.* On
the next page (127) are the figures:

$$1 \quad 2 \quad 3 \quad 4 \quad 5 \quad 6 \quad 7 \quad 8$$
$$2$$
$$\overline{}$$
$$2 \quad 4 \quad 6 \quad 8$$

Continuing, with the notebook upside down, toward the
front (p. 128): *In my rambles through the country of
the* [unfinished]. The entries then begin on page 124.
Returning from the back to the front, the fly-leaf (p. 5),
now upside down: *Thats the best road but the —— takes
ye doon a wee bit road & then ye gae doon the ——* [two
words illegible]. After this the figures:

$$1 \quad . \quad 19. \quad 6$$
$$1$$
$$1$$
$$\overline{}$$
$$3 \qquad 19. \quad 6$$
$$1 \qquad 8 \quad 6$$
$$\overline{}$$
$$2 \quad . \quad 11 \quad 0$$

On the inside front cover, upside down: *pay for Preston
—— [two words illegible]. send trunk ——* [two words

illegible]. *coat enquire about Professors Lodgings*   M^r
A. Sheriff —— Leith   [two words illegible].

```
        10
         3
         4
         1   6
        ───────
        18   6
         6   6
         3
        ───────
        28
```

Melrose castle   I paid 4 at —— [two words illegible]

```
        1.1  6
       10.   6
        1.   6
        1.   6
```

No other entries are on the outside front cover.

Volume II, read in the same fashion, has on the outside front cover: *1817 Miscellaneous notes during a tour
in Scotland with W^m C Preston.* On the inside front
cover, apparently in Irving's hand: *Most of the Memoranda in this book were made during a tour in Scotland
in 1817 in company with Wm C. Preston (since a senator
of the US).* Then follows in the hand of George Irving: *Memoranda made by Washington Irving Sunnyside
presented to me by my cousin Mrs P. M. Irving January
1885. George Irving.* Regular entries begin on page 1.
Continuing to the end, page 115 has been used as a fly-
leaf. It has the following expense account:

Balnaguard Inn	*10*	
Aberfeldie	*6.½*	*16.½*
Kenmore	*8.½*	*23*
Kirk of —— [three words illegible]	*8.½*	*31½*
——	*4.½*	*35*
——	*— 3.*	*38*
Killin	*1.*	*39*
Loch earn head Inn	*8.*	*47*
Callander —	*13.¾*	*60.*

At bottom of the page: *Dunkeld 5.9 —— 19.* On the reverse (116), nothing. On the back inside cover, a few obliterated words. On the back outside cover is a large letter S. Turning the book upside down and reading back toward the front, on the back outside cover, nothing is written; on the back inside cover: *£30.2-6.* Then follow a few words, all illegible except the interesting entry: *Coleridges new works Sybilline Leaves* [1817] *Biographia Literaria* [1817]. On the fly-leaf (p. 116), the only decipherable words are: *Capt. 2*^d *part of Murray Paris Prospectus Harrington Miss Edgeworth Works of Hume Hooker.* No other words on fly-leaves or covers are legible.

INDEX

*Five hundred and twenty-five copies
of this book have been printed for
Yale University Press. October, 1927.
Typography by Carl Purington Rollins,
Printer to Yale University.*
No. 403